World Class Brands

WORLD CLASS BRANDS

BRANDS

Chris Macrae

ADDISON-WESLEY PUBLISHING COMPANY

Wokingham, England · Reading, Massachusetts · Menlo Park, California
New York · Don Mills, Ontario · Amsterdam · Bonn · Sydney
Singapore · Tokyo · Madrid · San Juan · Milan · Paris
Mexico City · Seoul · Taipei

Many of the product or corporate names and logos mentioned in this book are claimed as trademarks.
A list of brand names commences on p. 189.

Cover designed by Hybert Design and Type, Maidenhead using photographs provided by Thunder & Colt
and Virgin Atlantic and printed by The Riverside Printing Co. (Reading) Ltd.
Typeset by Colset Private Limited, Singapore in 11/13½ Trump Medieval.
Printed in Great Britain by The Bath Press, Avon.

First printed 1991.

British Library Cataloguing in Publication Data
Macrae, Chris
World class brands.
1. Sales promotion
I. Title
658.827

ISBN 0-201-54407-5

Library of Congress Cataloging in Publication Data
Macrae, Chris.
World class brands / Chris Macrae.
p. cm.
Includes bibliographical references (p.) and indexes.
ISBN 0-201-54407-5
1. Brand name products. 2. Marketing. I. Title.
HD69.B7M33 1991   91-9557
658.8'27 — dc20   CIP

Prelude

The brand has travelled a long way this century: from the mark of a local product to a global corporate symbol. It has been the brainchild of our era of mass communications. More precisely, the brand and this era have been interdependent. How could newspapers, television programming or satellite transmission of international sporting events have flourished without the brand as their primary fund-raiser? Would capitalism have been any more successful than communism without the brand?

This book asks what will happen to the brand over the next 20 years or so. In spite of past successes, many large brands are now suffering from something of an identity crisis. Recently, the phrase 'think global, act local' has become marketing's most popular cliché, precisely because most brands began the other way round. Many would-be global brands grew up in multinational regimes where the approach was 'think local, act global only if local circumstances permit'.

Fortunately, global marketers do have some examples to look up to. Many are corporate brands. Among these, Coca-Cola is not only a world class organization, but its name is also probably the single most commonly understood entry in the universal dictionary of mankind.

Promotions directed at a worldwide stage (instead of a local one) often involve very original organizational practices. The range of effects can be illustrated by a select preview: McDonald's global celebrations of its opening in Moscow (page 25); Nestlé's focal use of Disney promotions to publicize food products throughout Europe over the next decade –'Instead of having a thousand new ideas, you can concentrate on just one' says Nestlé's director of visual communications (pages 46–8);

The Body Shop's expansion of its image through franchises located in the world's most modern shopping arcades; the statement of multiracial harmony which you can vote for by joining 'the United Colours of Benetton' (pages 27–30); Coke's born-again climax to its own centenary (pages 19–20).

Our search for ways in which world class brands are being organized will examine how often the ambition to be a world class company is incorporated with the brand's promise to the consumer. I shall introduce frameworks for testing whether a brand is communicating with worldly consistency to all of its audiences. Please test my generalizations against your personal experiences. In marketing it has always been important to 'what-if' the future. With world class brands management responsibility is reaching its ultimate state. Over the next decade, will we meet the alarming spectacle of a brand image which is assessed to represent a billion dollars of goodwill one day, and nothing a day later? Probably. The Branded Tree of Life (Chapter Nine) invites managers to track down the weakest links on which entire branding strategies – and their companies – depend.

For many business commentators, global branding has already been guilty of several false starts. A lot of things need to come together for it to make sense for a business to prioritize itself – its images and its organization – as globally singular rather than locally multiple. Trends which accelerated during the late eighties mean that many large companies have swung the balance of their interests towards transnational marketing for the first time. These include: focused investment to be a world leader in a few industries rather than a local player in many industries; the test marketing of a transnational marketplace proposed by the European Community (with added interest from events in Eastern Europe); the recognition that the historic structure of many multinationals has encouraged branders to research local consumer differences rather than transnational commonalities. In the long run, brands represent the levels at which a corporation chooses to advertise itself. Once an organization is geared to transnational merchandising, the last thing a company wishes to market competitively is a local brand, unless consumers really want to continue paying for its customization.

It is time to explore where world class brands will make sense.

ACKNOWLEDGEMENTS

To:

- Norman Macrae, my father and lead writer for *The Economist* over four decades, for helping to improve this text
- Former colleagues at Novaction (Paris), for the opportunity to evaluate brand positionings in over 40 countries
- Current colleagues at The Marketing Consultancy, Coopers & Lybrand Deloitte (London), for advancing the management precept of the brand as a fundamental source of competitive advantage
- Marketers from leading transnational companies for an unusual collection of insights on creative branding practices
- Consumers, without whose interviews, none of the nuances of branding would be meaningful (for example, the mother's reaction to a commercial for a nutritional children's food: 'frankly, instead of trying to sell me an idea that I already believe in, this would be a better brand if it helped me to sell the idea to my child')

Many Thanks

Chris Macrae
April 1991

Contents

Publisher's Acknowledgements

The author and publisher would like to thank the following for permission to reproduce copyright material on the cited pages:

Page 15: quote reproduced from Kenichi Ohmae © (1990) *The Borderless World*, William Collins & Co. Pages 15, 78 and 161–2: quotes reproduced from Akio Morita © (1986) *Made in Japan*, E.P. Dutton. Pages 16–17 and 19: quotes reproduced from Palazzini, F. © (1989) *Coca-Cola Superstar*, Columbus Books. Page 18: illustration reproduced by kind permission © The Coca-Cola Company, Atlanta, Georgia. Page 21: illustration reproduced by kind permission © Shiseido, London. Page 23: quote reproduced from Morgan, H. (1987) *Symbols of America* © Penguin Books USA Inc. Page 25: illustration reproduced by kind permission © Rex Features Ltd. Pages 25–6: quote reproduced from an article by Mary Dejevsky in *The Times* 25 January 1990 © Times Newspapers Ltd 1990. Pages 26–7, 29–30: quote reproduced from *The Economist* 3–9 February 1990 © The Economist. Page 30: illustration reproduced by kind permission © Benetton Group SpA. Page 35: quote reproduced from *Marketing* 24 May 1990 © Haymarket Marketing Publications Ltd. Page 36: quote reproduced from Reeves, R. © (1986) *Advertising Reality*, A.A. Knopf. Pages 38–9: quote reproduced from Watkins, J.L. © (1959) *The 100 Greatest Advertisements*, Dover. Page 39: illustrations reproduced by kind permission of General Mills, Inc., Minneapolis. Page 41: quote reproduced from Young, J.W. © (1963) *How to Become an Advertising Man*, Advertising Publications. Pages 46–8 and 92–3: quotes reproduced from *Euromarketing* 16 January 1990 © Crain Communications Inc. Page 47: illustration reproduced by kind permission © Daniel Kirk. Pages 53–4: quote reproduced from *The Financial Times* 1 November 1990 © The Financial Times Ltd. Page 61: quote reproduced from *The Independent on Sunday* 25 February 1990 by kind permission © George Bull. Page 64: quote reproduced from an article by Barry Day in *Marketing Week* © Centaur Communications Ltd. Page 65: quote reproduced from *The Economist* 10–16 November 1990 © The Economist. Page 66: illustration reproduced by kind permission © Esso Petroleum. Page 73: quote reproduced from Australia's *Marketing* October 1989 © John M. Bester & Associates Pty. Ltd. Page 79: quote reproduced from *Marketing Week* 24 November 1989 © Centaur Communications Ltd. Page 88: illustration reproduced by kind permission © La Chemise Lacoste Company, Paris. Pages 90–1: quote reproduced from Murphy, J.M. (ed) © (1987) *Branding – A Key Marketing Tool*, Macmillan Publishers. Page 94: quote reproduced from an article by Meredith Etherington Smith in the

Daily Telegraph 3 January 1988 © The Daily Telegraph. Pages 94–6: quote reproduced from Morton, A. © (1989) *Theirs is the Kingdom*, Michael O'Mara Books Ltd. Pages 96–7: quote reproduced from an article by Stuart Warell in *The Sunday Times* 9 September 1990 © Times Newspapers Ltd 1990. Pages 98–9: quote reproduced from an article by David Robson in *The Sunday Times* © Times Newspapers Ltd 1990. Page 101: quote reproduced from *International Management* August 1990 © Reed Business Publishing Group. Page 102: quote reproduced from *Campaign* 24 October 1990 © Haymarket Marketing Publications Ltd. Pages 102–4 and 151–2: quote reproduced from an article by Ian Fraser in *The Independent on Sunday* 28 January 1990 © The Independent. Page 104: quote reproduced from Harrison, A. © (1987) *Handbook of Advertising Techniques*, Kogan Page. Pages 104–5: quote reproduced from Olins, W. © (1989) *Corporate Identity*, Thames & Hudson. Page 135: quote reproduced from Watkins, J.L. © (1959) *The 100 Greatest Advertisements*, Dover. Page 136: illustration reproduced by kind permission © R.J. Reynolds Tobacco Company, Winston-Salem, North Carolina. Page 146: illustration of Landor ImagePower Survey™ 1988 reproduced by kind permission © Landor Associates and Companies. Individual logos are copyright of the companies concerned. Pages 147–8: quote reproduced from an article by Deirdre Fernand and Margaret Park in *The Sunday Times* 4 February 1990 © Times Newspapers Ltd 1990. Pages 152–3: quote reproduced from an article by Philip Jacobson and Janic Dettmer in *The Times* 14 February 1990 © Times Newspapers Ltd 1990. Pages 155–6: quote reproduced from Waterman, R. © (1987) *The Renewal Factor*, Bantam. Pages 165–7: quote reproduced from an article by Peter Drucker in *The Economist* 21 October 1989 © The Economist. Page 172: illustration reproduced by kind permission © Shell International Petroleum Company Limited, London. Page 173: quote reproduced from an article by Rupert Pennant-Rea in *The Economist* 5 May 1990 © The Economist. Pages 175–6: quote reproduced from *Marketing Week* 7 September 1990 © Centaur Communications Ltd.

OUT-TAKES

In compiling this book we were surprised that two pictures were 'censored' by their corporate owners:

- The reluctant cowboy (page 67): apparently Philip Morris' current policy is not to allow any publisher to reproduce the Marlboro icon.
- Oh my Darlie (page 56): we understood Colgate's sensitivity about the negro stereotype employed historically by Darkie toothpaste, but were reassured to hear that the brand was being popularly reborn as Darlie. Our offer to portray the before and after images of this achievement was rejected.

The reader will have noticed my fascination with branding metamorphosis. It seemed fitting to end with the story of the crocodile and the alligator. As the book was going to press, I received an urgent call from my publisher 'Lacoste

say they are a crocodile and not the alligator you refer to on page 88'. I'm as falli-
ble as the next consumer and no naturalist but according to my archives:

- Rene Lacoste was a French tennis player and a hero in Davies Cup competi-
  tions of the twenties. Lacoste acquired the nickname of the alligator and one
  of the world's most successful trademarks was born when a friend
  embroidered an alligator on the blazer he wore on the courts.

As a souvenir we retained the text's reference to the alligator while accepting
that today's consumer awareness is more popularly associated with crocodiles.

Global Framework, Local Action

Introduction

This book examines the fusion of two current business practices: the purposes communicated by organizations which wish to be world class competitors, and the rationales for investing in brands. These are more than costly business decisions. They are setting directions for people's lifestyles everywhere.

The world class brand is a natural resource for corporations faced with trends towards unification in the business world. For better or for worse, and both kinds of social impact are likely, the world class brand is a logical reflection of the fact that the companies which win at marketing are those which plan ahead of the competition.

Many business strategists now anticipate a converging world market for consumer goods and services, with transnational marketplaces like the European Community providing intermediate stepping stones. They are therefore intent on making themselves world class companies with world class brands.

This will be an exercise with swaying fortunes. Successful firms will need to achieve so many sorts of balance; between seeking economies of scale and meeting strictly local consumer needs; between appealing to lasting sets of customer values (such as parenthood and nature) and to rapidly changing sorts of consumer lifestyles; between a world class branding strategy which merits the incorporation of billions of dollars of goodwill and a local brand which is freer to select the customers it targets.

Today, as the world's most costly business strategies are being planned, many of the conventional rules of branding need reappraisal. My aim will be to explore the core missions that world class brands will serve and the mistakes to avoid as their marketplaces change. Let us begin with a panorama of the issues that confront the world class brand.

The mediator of our times

A brand has mutual responsibilities as a corporate ambassador and as a consumable possession.

As a communications vehicle for a company, a brand aims to establish a balance between two kinds of impression: the value of its offer (that is, making that next sale); and the quality of its credentials (that is, advancing its reputation for the company among such varied audiences as shareholders, employees, customers, suppliers, government and society).

Among brands with world class standing, typical members such as Coca-Cola, Disney, McDonald's or Sony incorporate billions of dollars of goodwill and feed on hundreds of millions of dollars per annum to maintain their status. This breed of brand needs to be sensitive to global standards of accountability.

As a consumable possession, all brands aim to become habit-forming by pre-empting particular associations in customers' minds. The stock-in-trade is empathy. A brand which I choose to consume regularly on social occasions can become as much a part of my image as the clothes I wear. The brand which is a private indulgence can serve an important human need – the affirmation that I am being true to my character and beliefs.

The strongest of branded communications build consistently on an inspirational direction. A brand like Rolls-Royce benefits from decades of following David Ogilvy's guiding principle – build the brand image for people to wear, and through this process become part of the fabric of life.

At the start of our broadcasting age, even advertising gurus like David Ogilvy would have needed the gifts of a prophet to foresee the familiarity that world class brands have now achieved. In a worldwide poll, many of today's most famous names are brands. Being world class is to appeal as a constant reference point in a world where lesser things are changing rapidly.

If consumers believe that a brand sets the world class standard, there is an opportunity to motivate company employees in the same pursuit of excellence. Advertising British Airways as the 'World's Favourite Airline' was a powerful way of seeding this symbiotic reaction. By translating the new corporate badge into a mission of pride for staff to act on every day, management has put this formerly stodgy nationalized business into privatized lift-off. Thus can a branded corporate image grow into a reality.

A billion-dollar brand evaporates into a wasteful exercise unless all of a company's audiences recognize their share in its credibility. This is one reason why the company as a brand is a superior strategy, provided the product-and-people portfolios fit. Japanese companies are masters at this; so are an increasing number of entrepreneurial franchise operations ranging from Hilton Hotels to The Body Shop boutiques.

Cadbury Schweppes is a Western packaged-goods company which is making it look easy to mature as twin corporate brands. The drinks stream Schweppes is happy to enter any suitable venture which builds up world class production capacity and bottling distribution channels. While local businesses may be acquired to consolidate the company's mission to be one of the world's top three soft drinks companies ranked alongside Coca-Cola and Pepsi-Cola, the branded strategy is to put the Schweppes badge on every drink that is 'dry'.

Dry is a world class position – imagewise and productwise – providing an interesting repertoire of credentials to communicate such as slimline, adult flavours, and socially non-alcoholic. The word also helps to recall the refreshing reason for needing a drink while ringing sharply, simply and sexily off international tongues. Schweppes marketers can take pride in growing this segment of the soft drinks market with popular new dry flavours complementing such global classics as Schweppes Indian Tonic Water and Canada Dry Ginger Ale.

In tandem with Schweppes, Cadbury's, one of the world's top five confectionery companies (along with Mars, Hershey's, Nestlé, and Jacobs Suchard), is equally committed to branding our taste buds. As the first name in chocolate in many British

Commonwealth countries, Cadbury's is actively seeking joint ventures to extend its 'menu of chocolate' from confectionery to cakes, biscuits, milk drinks, liqueurs and whatever entrepreneurial production in tune with modern consumer appetites may bring.

Unlike Cadbury Schweppes, many Western conglomerates have entered the nineties with portfolios comprising several hundred separately identified brands. The design of umbrella identities for marrying these brands into world class families is one of the management approaches to transnational marketing which we will meet in later chapters.

A successful world class brand should command a position that will continuously increase the number of people who can feel proud to be associated with it. Marketing history already shows that brands with heritages of good faith have the power to transcend generations and national frontiers in our era of converging global communications.

Global headlines have certain risks

Fame and the high international standards expected of world class brands make them natural candidates for global news headlines. Like superstars, megabrands own the hallmarks which journalists revel in:

- They have differentiated themselves as the world's number one in something (even if *they* have defined what this is).

- They offer stereotype images which can be used in international copy with few words of introduction to the reader.

- As celebrities they are fair prey for public scrutiny where the ground rules of the popular media are passive adoration of success and 'rotweiller' investigation into failure. Branded contradictions can be as naggingly self-destructive as human scandals.

Owners of world class brands should plan for changes in the image which are gradual and private rather than abrupt and public. This puts a premium on an appetite for what-iffing alternative future scenarios.

COKE'S CLASSIC FRIENDSHIP

Coca-Cola provides one of the most transparent histories of a brand as a communications ambassador. The message consolidated over a hundred years is that Coke is the right drink wherever friends meet. Branded drinks do not survive without a social image. Coca-Cola competes by pre-empting the position of the international friend whom everyone can rely on.

Coke, the brand, has even taught its own marketers a few lessons in consistency. When a new marketing team propositioned the United States of America with a Bold New Coke for the eighties, consumers voted No until the Real Thing was reinstated. Few marketing performances have attracted such coverage as the day Coca-Cola blinked. Several books have become popular testimonies to the occasion.

Lessons from Coke's diversion include:

- Brands develop clans of supporters. The market leader has the most to gain from this, with loyal consumers cheering on its progress – and congratulating each other on their mutually discerning taste. The world class brand invites consumers to belong to a global club. Among parity products, being seen to be the consistent leader of a popular experience is the real appeal.

- The escape route for Coke's overbold marketers was to let the brand make a triumphant return. Since they bravely took the rap for their mistake, the Coca-Cola legend seems set to continue, with the suggestion that, while marketers are only mortal, the brand is immortal.

CITIZEN OR CYNIC, GLOBALLY MEDIATED

World class brands, as the most public faces of international corporations, are drawing an increasing share of media attention. This trend will accelerate as parochial news barons are being replaced by transnational news merchandisers.

World class brands need to be carefully positioned to exploit the media's appetite for glossy business stories palatable for international consumption. Readers' local reactions matter. The *opportunity* is to be seen to be growing up as a leading global citizen; the *risk* is to be increasingly badmouthed as a cynical commercial facade.

Converging marketplaces

The European Community, as a concept for a transnational marketplace, has promoted an irreversible trend in international business thinking. Previously, large European companies could afford to grow brands wherever local businesses seemed most accessible. Henceforth, a focused international business strategy appears more attractive. Focused planning involves concentrating investment in businesses where the company can operate in Europe's top division, while selling off local businesses which do not fit this pattern.

This rationale for focused strategies in Europe stems from a fact of life in national marketplaces. Brand leaders are usually very profitable enterprises, while other brands frequently make only marginal contributions to international companies. Retail chains, wherever they are dominant, have increasingly squeezed out minor brands.

In the European Community, advertising experts like John Banks, UK chairman of Young & Rubicam, foresee the day when 'one market means in effect the same brand leader and two or three significant players in all European markets'. European players who share this kind of thinking believe in focusing their business strategies.

Pan-European branders may not be able to stop there. Being in the world's top division in an industry appears to be the safest way of retaining corporate independence. This corporate viewpoint is reinforced by the long-term scenario that a triad of transnational marketplaces will emerge: Japan (with rising Asian suns), the Americas (North and South) and the Europes (West and East). It is becoming hard for a manufacturing company to see how to survive independently as a leading brander in just one of these regions.

Europe's convergence – retailwise, mediawise and consumer-wise – might extend over decades, but transnational companies must plan for where future trends are leading rather than for more immediate eventualities. Ownership of world class brands is becoming a necessary each-way bet for all companies that can afford the investment which a global focus implies.

The UCU – Unique Competitive Umbrella

Different leagues of branding require different management practices. I suggest that businesses are only beginning to understand the real competitive advantages of brand equity in the world class division. We can symbolize the issues to be debated by borrowing from a flag of Europe's single marketplace to coin the acronym UCU – standing for Unique Competitive Umbrella. The corporate purposes of branding a UCU are depicted in Figure 1.1. While the left-side characteristics of a brand – as a consumer

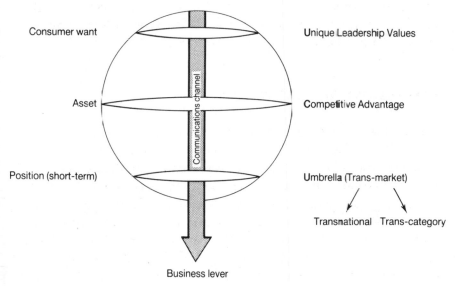

Figure 1.1 Branding – the UCU.

want, as an asset, and as a short-term position – are widely accepted, the right-side property rights of branding a UCU can easily get lost in complex organizational processes. Consider the practical implications of each of these property rights.

UNIQUE LEADERSHIP VALUES

Can leadership values be branded by a literal implementation of the market research process as collecting data to target what consumers say they want? I have found consulting for Japanese companies to be an eye-opening experience because they use market research to test hunches rather than to help form them. The Japanese are formidable branders because consensus gives the special advantage that the CEO, the brand manager, the market researcher and the R&D technologist take mental turns in wearing each other's hats. Witness Sony's leadership values epitomized by CEO Akio Morita in rejecting a market research suggestion that the Walkman could not be viable: 'Our plan is to lead the public rather than ask them what kind of product they want. The public does not know what is possible, but we do'.

This practical mission is also a necessary one if the brand's image as a leader is to be conceived as building the goodwill of all those audiences which interact with a brand's communications channel between business and consumer.

COMPETITIVE ADVANTAGE

Standard textbooks on business strategy do not fully appreciate the UCU's potential as a source of competitive advantage. Strategic frameworks devised before 'brand valuation' became an item for boardroom agendas fail to allow for the fact that some brands provide leverage opportunities across marketplaces. Consequently, planning scenarios on market entry barriers can be turned upside down. For example, two summers ago, the UK ice cream manufacturer, Lyons Maid, could reflect with pleasure on the maturity of its marketplace and the particularly high entry barriers involving freezer distribution. Today, the business is up for sale melting under the competitive pressure of the extension of Mars' equity from a chocolate bar to ice cream.

UMBRELLA (TRANS-MARKET CULTURES)

The classic brand management system – one product, one brand – is passing into history. Leading consumer goods multi-nationals, owning hundreds of separate brands, are finding themselves 'over-branded' – with too many marginal communications channels – given that the megatrends of branding include: escalating media costs, retailer own-branding and the change from a parochial to an international world. All products have lifecycles. Umbrella brands need not have; instead they can be ageless lifestyles provided their franchise is the animation of a durable culture. Umbrella branding is not easy because of the short-term pressures which are an undercurrent of any business organization. Yet we will see that Unique Competitive Umbrellas do exist and being in the world class league brings the added advantage that other organizations want to work under your umbrella.

Management dimensions for branding strategies

I am not suggesting that every small firm should want to market world class brands, but I do suggest that branded excellence will become increasingly polarized. On the one hand, all companies will continue to profit from timely matching of products with local needs. On the other hand, transnational companies will need to embrace a marketing philosophy which balances the need to organize around world class options with the targeting of local niches. Even the most dedicated local company may find that a time comes when it needs either to defend its marketplace from world class competition or to make an alliance with such a competitor.

For marketers used to brands which target gaps in local markets, the insidious threat from the world class brand is its power to make a marketing virtue out of breadth. When competing against an international brand, useful strategic clues often come from separating its local faces, and asking what gives its international heart a marketing edge.

Figure 1.2 suggests dimensions which present constantly changing opportunities and risks for any branded investment. The world class aim changes the levels of balance which need to be struck. Across most dimensions, strategic priorities tend to move from left to right as market leaders shift from locally targeted selling to globally integrated marketing.

QUICK SALE VERSUS QUALITY MISSION

In the naked world of commodity products we buy on price; in the dressed-up world of brands we aspire to, though may not always be able to afford, the brand with the best image of quality. Compare the reputations of Woolworths with Marks & Spencer, or Amstrad with Sony. The difference can be perceived as marketing to a price or to a quality standard.

World class brands lead the quality standard and avoid the price war. While cost-effectiveness is an essential part of any marketing strategy, those who brand their marketing edge as price limit their future margins for manoeuvre in adding global value.

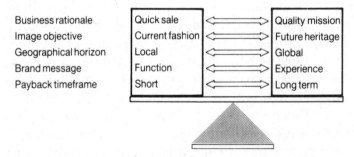

Figure 1.2 Business balances for investments in brands.

CURRENT FASHION VERSUS FUTURE HERITAGE

In our media-influenced world, where even scientists now pose as guardians against possibly non-existent global warming to be currently newsworthy, world class heritages provide a contrast by touching us with a homely constancy. Positioning commitments to such values as parenthood, good health or a royal sense of taste demonstrate a substance which is above the whim of fashion and beyond the journalist's red pen.

World class brands may use fashionable faces to compete, but above all they have a confidence to lead the future from a heritage rooted in sincerely working for a positive good

LOCAL VERSUS GLOBAL

Brands seldom engender world class spirit without being sure of their own nationalities. There are two contrasting communications styles. The *touristically ethnic* plays on an accepted international stereotyping of a nation's image while steering clear of any national warts. The *supranational* tunes into a universal sense of excellence which touches people irrespective of race or creed. Both types of brand aim to steer clear of issues concerning specifically national passions.

The local brand is less concerned about its international image. In fact, it often protects its marketplace by playing on locally chauvinistic traits which establish its authority to identify with a local audience.

Most worldly consumers enjoy choosing between both kinds of experience.

FUNCTION VERSUS EXPERIENCE

World class brands add atmosphere to the world of functional products. They service lifestyles, act as props in human role-playing, provide status symbols or transform a social experience into a memorable event. A brand which shares globally identified credentials with purchasers, consumers and witnesses offers a badge to be worn, an invitation to join a universal club.

World class brands are characters in an experiential language whose global presence in the mind depends on the consistency and uniform visibility with which a brand makes particular values its own. Turning a product into an experience is an investment in time and money. The local brander often prefers a hard sell on product functions which may have measurable effectiveness from the outset.

SHORT-RANGE VERSUS LONG-TERM

A company cannot afford to build a brand with a world class reputation unless its image is going to transcend generations. Over-commitment to the growth of too many world class images can cause a multinational a loss of focus which can be just as serious as operating with too many product categories.

Branding – May the force of non-fragmentation be with you

Good marketing involves facilitating offers that are as customized as technology and human endeavour can manage, while maintaining an economic balance which satisfies the customer and the company. Branding provides the power to identify a cause which unites people over time – with an appeal that acts as a centre of gravity – so that customers can benefit from economies of scale while enjoying a feeling of individual attention.

If I have chosen the words of that last paragraph carefully enough, you should feel that branders – who are the most costly image-makers of modern society – exercise an enormous responsibility. On the one hand it is wasteful to construct a brand solely as a fragmenter which will carve out a business with increasingly limited opportunities; on the other hand it is exploitative to attempt to blow up a cause which has little merit. Fortunately, advertising history already shows that such hot-air strategies rebound over the long term, to the public discredit of the enterprises that have floated them.

Branding's united nations

Today, the world class priority is a natural focus for transnational companies faced with convergent marketplaces. World class brands can provide the characters of a common language which aim to touch many culturally different people. The best of them will need to mediate between societies where it is trendy to feel environmentally guilty of conspicuous consumption and countries where folk are only just aspiring to the worldwide status symbols of free competitive markets.

Many big companies are at a global crossroads where identities of worldwide repute may endorse a multiplicity of products, but where one false note can spoil a symphony. Mixing the right names with the right businesses will ensure companies a place on the world stage for well into the next century; over-opportunistic or misleading identifications of products will destroy some of today's largest business empires.

The power of the brand is to mix image with reality. Most consumers now enjoy having a mixture of local and international offerings at their front doors. Appeals to our local senses remind us of our roots, offers of international experiences broaden our horizons. In John Naisbitt's words, this is one of the megatrends for our third millennium: the blend of 'global lifestyles and cultural nationalism'.

Most employees are motivated by the esteem in which their company is held. When you contribute to products which are universally acknowledged as leaders of the quality standard, the joys of excellence range from the intangible pride of being a winner, to the transparent approval of peers. Your social circles widen and your local community expands. Brands as corporate flagships should be used as guides to heightening the spirit of working life.

Take a trip to the Orient for two examples.

Our first stopover is Tokyo. Much has been written about Japanese corporate man, his practice of consensus and the prime importance of the company to his way of life. At work, the Sony man simply would not do anything which is unSony-like. Sony quality becomes a matter of the care you take if you see yourself as part of the Sony family. This is the company working as a brand at its most powerful. The bond between the company and the outside world, through employee–product–service–trade–consumer–society, is communicated, almost ritually, by means of the corporate symbol. Product lines are seldom advertised on Japanese television without clear identification of the corporate symbol which warrants it. Almost subliminally, the Japanese consumer vets new products for their corporate status. Reciprocally, the esteem in which the corporate badge is held throughout the community returns to be the pride of the individual employee.

Our second stopover is Singapore. Yesterday's big cities generally grew up around their trading links as ports. Singapore deserves credit for being the first place to aim singlemindedly to be the number one airport destination in the world.

The Singapore communications strategy, with its airline as its commercial flagship, has long been an example of branded excellence. The slogan 'Singapore girl – you're a great way to fly' is almost legendary. It has provided the image for a tourist and businessmen's centre of gravity in the Far East around which the servicing infrastructure has been relentlessly built. For example, Singapore innovated the idea that an airport should be an attractive place and had the confidence to charge travellers for this privilege. Today, Singapore has arrived as Asia's late-century New York, giving its citizens every bit as much pride in what they have built as New Yorkers must have had in the twenties.

Some people are tempted to look down on Singapore's image-building by querying its sexism. They should answer two questions. Do they think that Singaporeans would enjoy the advantages they now have if their airline had been marketed like an Aeroflot? What right do they have to criticize an emblem of hope and beauty which was designed as a statue of liberty in our mass-communications age?

The world's best products often depend on highly personal commitments. Local products of excellence will always be prized, but in an era where the meanings of local and national boundaries will soon need to be questioned more honestly, world class brands should have the confidence and the integrity to symbolize the best produce, services and experiences which transnational cooperatives have to offer.

Again, the fast track to this global vision comes from tapping into Japanese lines of thought. Here is Kenichi Ohmae – on people, countries and transnational trade – in his book *The Borderless World*, followed by Akio Morita of Sony on world class organization.

Kenichi Ohmae:

- People are global when as consumers they have access to information about goods and services from around the world.

- The prosperity of countries depends on their ability to create value through their people and not by husbandry of resources and technologies. . . . If you look at the prosperous nations today – Switzerland, Singapore, Taiwan, South Korea and Japan – they are characterised by small land mass, no resources, and well-educated hardworking people who all have the ambition to participate in the global economy.

- An isle is emerging that is bigger than a continent – the Interlinked Economy (ILE) of the Triad (the United States, Europe and Japan) joined by aggressive economies such as Taiwan, Hong Kong and Singapore. It is becoming so powerful that it has swallowed most consumers and corporations, made traditional borders almost disappear, and pushed bureaucrats, politicians and the military towards the status of declining industries.

Akio Morita:

Only truly global companies can achieve "global localisation", that is, be as much of an insider as a local company but still accomplish benefits of world-scale operations.

Hesitantly, we may go forward with the credo that the world class brand – worthy of the name as well as the investment of up to a billion dollars of goodwill – should be nurtured to thrive as the mediator of our times. It should unite a company's people and its global audiences in a succession of warming experiences, while maintaining a proper marketing balance between valuable local offers and a worldwide reputation for quality.

Four Exemplary World Class Brands

Coca-Cola

Robert Woodruff was Coca-Cola's mentor for most of the twentieth century. His definition for the brand's marketing mission was 'to be within arm's reach of desire' around the world. This has had a fundamental effect on Coca-Cola's operational strategy. At the first sniff of a new market, the company's reflex reaction is distributive. No investment is spared to have the first and best bottling network in place. The most amazing coup of distribution made on behalf of any branding came with America's entry into the Second World War. Woodruff immediately issued the directive that, regardless of the cost to the company, Coca-Cola would go wherever American GIs went at a cost of five cents a bottle. Woodruff was so convincing on Coca-Cola's powers as a morale booster that America's war office contributed significantly to the investments in bottling plants that Coca-Cola needed to be the GIs mascot. Palazzini, author of *Coca-Cola Superstar*, takes up the story:

> Woodruff took care to justify the need for his drink to be in the daily ration of the troops, through a written document to the government with the meaningful title "The importance of relaxation in the supreme fatigue of war". Obviously, in the foreground was Coca-Cola, the "pause that refreshes", symbol of civilian life at home.
>
> Once he got the go-ahead, Woodruff assembled a team of technicians, "Coca-Cola Colonels", whose duties were to make

sure that no soldier went without his Coca-Cola; not even in the most inaccessible place or where the battle was fiercest. Overcoming the most incredible difficulties of transport and supply, the men managed to meet their target. By the end of the war, five billion bottles had been consumed.

But Coca-Cola did more than help troop morale – in many places it gave the local people their first taste of Coca-Cola, and it was a taste most liked. It put the company in position to take a giant leap forward. In 1940 Coca-Cola was bottled in 44 countries; by 1960 the figure had more than doubled and Coca-Cola had become a symbol of peace the world over.

As far back as 1911, Coca-Cola's advertising budget first exceeded a million dollars. A good product alone could never have afforded such visibility. The password for Coca-Cola's function was 'refreshing', its 1904 slogan being 'the most refreshing drink in the world'. But the image link which kept the brand apart from others was its emotional appeal as the socially acceptable drink. Only once, late in its adolescence as its commercial fame was soaring, did Coca-Cola come near to being spoilt by its success.

Coca-Cola had enjoyed the natural good fortune of being born (1886) into the right social circles. While Victorian Britons had their tea houses and the French had their cafés, American society had soda fountains. Coca-Cola soon became the standard drink of the soda fountain set. Until Coca-Cola was into its teens as a product, the only way to participate in the Coca-Cola experience was by sharing it in such genteel company.

In 1899, Asa Candler (the proprietor of Coca-Cola) was approached by two young men, Thomas and Whitehead, who wanted the concession to bottle Coca-Cola. The idea seemed distant from the core business which Candler had nurtured. He surrendered the right to bottle Coca-Cola in the USA for the peppercorn royalty of one dollar.

Over the next decade, it was distribution in the bottle which developed the product's mass public. In doing so it spawned a rash of competitors. As well as Pepsi, Palazzini's list of colas of the time cites the likes of Cola Congo, Cola Sola, Cola Kola, Cola Nova and Better Cola. Surrounded by imitators in name and flavour, how was Coca-Cola to retain its unique identity?

Thomas's inspiration was that a very special bottle could be

The real feeling of a century of copywriters' fees.

the best resort for the brand's identity. He began in 1913 a competition to 'find a bottle that anyone would recognise even in the dark; a bottle unique in the whole world'. By 1915 Thomas's vision had been answered by a shape which has become the packaging industry's most famous offspring.

The evocative style of Coca-Cola's bottle came just in time to renew the unique social standing of the drink. Within a few years American society was to play into Coca-Cola's hands. Prohibition started. Coca-Cola was the one brand of drink which was properly attired in every sense.

Under Woodruff's careful guidance, Coca-Cola's once optimistic-sounding claim to be the most friendly drink in the world eventually became a commercial reality. A few snapshots illuminate the consistency of the process. In the thirties, when there was no tradition of a worker's coffee break, it was Coca-Cola that popularized the idea of a refreshment break and persuaded factory owners to install vending machines . . . during the Second World War, 'Big Red' became the soldier's friend and the friend of his loved ones back home . . . Coca-Cola is visible wherever tourists go, a friend however far you are from home . . . as the Berlin Wall crumbled, Coke made sure it was the first brand to be sampled by East German border-crossers (at one early checkpoint cans were given out at a rate of 10 000 per hour). If there is a pre-eminent commercial symbol of the American dream, Coke is it.

'Think big' seems to be the corporate motto of Coca-Cola. Yet even Coca-Cola's President Donald Keough admits to some doubts as to whether 'our system is going to handle 1992'. His calendar for the year is full of mega-events that offer pan-European marketing challenges: the Olympics in Barcelona and Albertville, the World Fair at Seville, the 500th anniversary of Columbus's voyage and the opening of France's Euro Disney-world, where Coke is the exclusive soft drink.

Ultimately, the resilience of Coca-Cola's image is a testimony to the investment in branding. Two examples help to show how an image superpower makes its own contribution to the popular history of our times.

By 1970, Vietnam had damaged America's image to the extent that being a part of the American dream was turning into an international liability. Coca-Cola's response was to declare a peace treaty in a way that no American president ever could. Here is how Coke's 'biographer' Palazzini tells this episode of Coke's history:

> In 1971 the famous "Hill Top" advertisement was simultaneously broadcast in all countries, achieving what young people aspired to – a world without frontiers. It showed young people in their national costumes representing 30 countries. Together in a group on a hillside, they sang the appealing jingle, "I'd like to buy the world a home, and furnish it with love, grow apple trees and honey bees and snow white turtle doves." And not for eight lines was Coca-Cola mentioned: . . . I'd like to buy the world a Coke.
>
> In the very first week the advertisement screened, more than 4000 letters of approval arrived in Atlanta from young people. The pop group, the New Seekers were licensed to make a non-commercial version of the jingle. It reached the top of the hit parade and royalties were donated to UNICEF. The ad appealed to all ages and established once and for all Coca-Cola's universal charisma.

In 1985, Coca-Cola had reached the age of 99. Behind the scenes we might have expected to see preparations being made for the imminent centenary. Actually, Coca-Cola's funeral was about to be staged. Keynotes from the play were these:

- Coke had been losing ground in American ratings to Pepsi's taste challenge and Michael Jackson's rapport with a new generation of consumers.
- A formulation for New Coke appeared to be a convincing favourite over the centenarian in taste tests where over 100 000 consumers were asked their preference (without knowing the names of either drink).
- In April 1985, Roberto Goizueta, Chairman of the Coca-Cola company, presented America with a 'bold New Coke for the Eighties'. The old Coca-Cola was to be withdrawn so that it would no longer exist that summer.
- Within a day, most Americans had heard the news and world press coverage had started. As each day went by, consumer reactions mounted. New stories circulated the world's media on America's cry to bring back the old Coca-Cola.
- The Coca-Cola company let the story rage for nearly 50 days before announcing that the old Coca-Cola would be reprieved and henceforth be known in America as Coca-Cola Classic.

There are features of this spectacle that are worth a second look. The Coca-Cola company achieved worldwide coverage of unprecedented commercial impact. The symbolic message was of a nation – the wealthiest nation – almost on its knees in a plea for the restoration of the old Coca-Cola. The legend continues with the suggestion that the image of Coca-Cola could not have gained more if everything had been planned this way. Could it?

As journalist Jess Meyers has observed:

> If the invention of a new Coca-Cola and the introduction into the market of the old Coke as a new product with the "classic" label is really the fruit of a well-studied advertising manoeuvre, then Machiavelli deserves to lose his place in history to Chairman Goizueta.

Shiseido

Among the world's top three cosmetics companies, the image of
Shiseido, with its perpetual sense of direction, is unlike any
other. Shiseido has an ethereal sense of feminity nurtured on the
coalescence of Eastern and Western imaginations.

Yushin Fukuhara founded Shiseido in 1872 in Tokyo's Ginza
district, where he opened the first Western-style pharmacy in
Japan. By 1888, Fukuhara's range of products included the first
toothpaste available in Japan, and his shop was being patronized
by Tokyo's high society. In catering for this trade, he soon moved
away from medicaments and towards beauty products.

In 1900, Fukuhara returned from a trip to the USA so
impressed by the concept of the American drugstore that he
opened a soda fountain counter. His shop became the place to
rendezvous and his decorative cosmetic products were revered
both as artistic symbols and as the progress of science towards
beauty.

In 1908 Yushin's son Shinzo left Japan to read pharmacology at
Columbia University (New York) and to tour Europe, where the
artistic culture of Paris made a fundamental impression on him.
Soon after returning to Tokyo, Shinzo took over as head of

Femininity *sans frontières*.

Shiseido. The credo which he put into practice was that business and culture should not be two separate domains foreign to one another. He saw them as twins which would grow only through mutual interaction. Under Shinzo's direction a design department was created within Shiseido, consisting of an élite mix of artists, writers and researchers. It was their responsibility to develop promotional materials for the company's products. One of the first fruits of their labour was the sign of the camellia which was to be branded on all Shiseido's products: a trademark which the company still uses today.

Shinzo believed that every Shiseido product should improve the image of the business. Through his expert scientific knowledge and his love of the artistic, he innovated quality products in a style which has become Shiseido's own.

The heritage of Shiseido is reflected today in the work of the company and the art of its foremost commercial designer, the Frenchman, Serge Lutens. His work is regularly awarded prizes by juries at international advertising congresses. It often pays to be cynical about the selling power of 'arty' advertising, but this does not apply to Shiseido where artistic merit is a living part of the product. Our portrait of Shiseido may be aptly concluded by noting what the French think of the brand. In a recent exhibition of Shiseido's products at the museum of advertising in Paris, the curator's brochure concluded:

> The name of Shiseido has a particular sense. It signifies: "the house which contributes to and facilitates a human way of living", and this signification finds its essence in a famous Japanese poem from the book on divine virtues by Ekikyo Kohka: "The virtue of the earth which we inherit is incomparable. This virtue of the earth combines with the virtue of the sky to collapse the boundary between what we do and what we imagine."

McDonald's

This is how Hal Morgan chronicles the birth of McDonald's in his encyclopaedic collection of brand biographies *The Symbols of America*:

The first McDonald's restaurant was opened in Pasadena, California, in 1937 by two brothers, Maurice and Richard McDonald. It sold hamburgers but otherwise bore little relation to the McDonald's we know today. In 1939 they opened a second stand in San Bernardino, and it was here that they gradually worked out the details and added the flourishes that would make the chain an international institution. By streamlining the kitchen operation, putting infra-red lamps over a food-holding area, and selling everything on a self-service basis, they were able to offer fast, cheap food. And by making the building a standing advertisement with two neon-lit, yellow arches sticking through the roof, they pulled in a constant stream of customers. (An even taller arch soared over the parking lot, with a hamburger-headed man named Speedy. He was retired in 1962.)

Ray Kroc was a fifty-two-year-old milkshake-mixer salesman when he came to San Bernardino to find out why the McDonald brothers needed eight of his machines. He was amazed at what he saw, and after two days of watching, he approached the brothers with an offer to sell their concept as a franchise. That was in 1954. By 1961 Kroc had licensed more than two hundred McDonald's restaurants, and that year he bought the brothers out for $2.7 million. By the time of his death in 1984, Kroc had expanded the chain to almost eight thousand outlets worldwide, and had made the golden arches an internationally recognized symbol of American enterprise.

McDonald's provides food for thought for those who claim that most famous brands need to be old-timers. Outside of America, McDonald's international fame was a popular phenomenon which accelerated fastest in the late seventies. Most famous brands are mixtures of old and new. Some parts of them may take the investment of generations to perfect. But ultimately, when everything comes together, successful growth and international acclaim often take place at an exponential rate.

In future, it would be a fair bet that most of the big new branded successes in a convergent world-marketplace will employ more of the franchisor's mechanisms of timely growth and less of the classical brander's all-or-nothing launches. The franchisor has the advantage that he tests his market as he goes; he receives feedback on improvements from traders who have his interests at heart. Therefore, the business has more opportunity to evolve at the brand's natural rate of growth.

The progress of McDonald's to the state we know today has involved three broad generations of development. The first was the working definition of a single fast-food site with the aim of customer satisfaction, which the McDonald family had clearly engineered by 1954. The second was the business genius of Ray Kroc in expanding the franchise statewide over the next quarter of a century. The third was the fine-tuning of an image to satisfy international consumption.

While the McDonalds clearly pioneered the fast-food product, they did not in my book invent the brand. A world of communications separates a popular local emporium from a chain-store image capable of supporting hundreds of outlets. What Ray Kroc identified was the emotional need for a consistently homely offer across the length and breadth of America's highways. The kind of offer that a stranger to town could take his family to in complete confidence.

McDonald's began to export its family-peace-of-mind successfully in the seventies. By this time a significant proportion of city dwellers everywhere found mobile mealtimes were part of their personal calendars. Not necessarily competing with a real meal, nor often the proper time for a meal break, but the relaxing experience of sitting-down-to-a-table or picnicking nonetheless. McDonald's offer is a modern-day equivalent of the 'pause which refreshes' – the citizen's timeout which Coca-Cola first institutionalized in the thirties. In world class branding, *plus ça change, plus c'est la même chose*.

Kroc's symbolic institution of 'Hamburger University' was a brilliant step. McDonald's depends on making a staff ritual out of those minimum standards of consistency that customers have a right to expect, day-in day-out from branch to branch across the globe. With a daily customer base of 23 million people, the fast-food business of McDonald's is a pioneer of the arrival of the factory floor at the point of mass consumption. At a personal level, the friendly face which McDonald's crews bring to this repetitive exercise is a remarkable compliment to the culture of the brand.

On longer range policy issues, McDonald's has developed equally remarkable organizational skills. In terms of planning integration as a good neighbour in foreign communities across the world, students of the Hamburger University might well claim to have studied some of the most practical problems ever encountered in a sociology degree.

Ultimately, the standards of McDonald's as a service leader may be tested even more demandingly than Ray Kroc could have anticipated. The McDonald's franchise looks like the kind of symbolic unit which an Eastern European public will personally equate with a fast test-market of capitalism in action. Here is Mary Dejevsky's report (for *The Times* of London) on McDonald's first day as a commercial ambassador in Moscow:

> A portion of the American dream came to Pushkin Square, Moscow, yesterday when the biggest McDonald's hamburger restaurant in the world made its debut for the press. To Western eyes it looked more or less like any other McDonald's. But Soviet journalists blinked when they went in. The cleanliness, the brightness, the space, the high chairs for the children. . . .
>
> Contemplating what she described as "this dazzling palace" one journalist said the secret of McDonald's would be harder for Russians to penetrate than the B-2 bomber.
>
> She was not far wrong. The McDonald's code is as distant from the realities of Soviet life as it is possible to be.
>
> Scarcely were we through the door than beaming young assistants, neatly uniformed, with badges saying "Can I help you?"

More than a global ambassador for fast food?

bounced up to offer order slips. There were young Russians running for burgers, crowded round the tills, sweeping the floor, polishing the tables and saying (in Russian): "Thank you for coming".

Twenty-year-old Marina, her smile thoroughly genuine, said she loved the work. Like many, she was a student, working about 15 hours a week – so introducing to Moscow another American notion, that of working your way through college.

. . .

The Moscow McDonald's story began 15 years ago when Mr George Cohon, president of McDonald's, Canada, started talks with the Russians. There were many hurdles; but now McDonald's has a purpose-built factory three quarters of an hour out of the city, built by foreigners to American standards. The company has its own cattle, potato fields and pasteurization equipment, and Western and Soviet "evaluators" work side by side, checking the French fries.

Some questions remain. To see young Russians dressed up as young Americans is suddenly to realise how unsophisticated and poorly nourished most of them look. And then, not everyone in Moscow favours Westernisation. McDonald's may have enemies.

When the Canadian managers and instructors have gone home, will the Soviet team be able to sustain their "dazzling palace" in this wilderness of mediocrity? With an estimated clientele of up to 15,000 people a day, queues are expected in Pushkin Square. But as Mr Cohon said: "The thing is that when they get to the end of the line, there is going to be food." If that promise alone is kept, it will make the Moscow McDonald's queue unique.

However, as *The Economist* observes, the costs of this kind of global PR are immense. We are getting to the stage where globally branded companies, like nations, may best be served by two sorts of governing bodies – executive managers in charge of business operations, and elder statesmen with the status and the time to engage in ambassadorial missions for the company:

True the symbolism is irresistible: the epitome of capitalist consumerism come to the citadel of world communism. But the extraordinary lengths to which McDonald's has had to go to open its Moscow outlet bodes ill for other companies hoping to reach the Soviet Union's 283m frustrated consumers.

Although the food and drink served by the Moscow restaurant

are indistinguishable from that served in McDonald's restaurants from Peoria to Tokyo, the company has had to alter radically the way it does business in order to achieve this feat. Rather than buying from local suppliers, as it does everywhere else, it has been forced to integrate vertically through the local food industry on a heroic scale, importing potato seeds and bull semen and indirectly managing dairy farms, cattle ranches and vegetable plots. It has also had to construct the world's largest food processing plant, the size of five soccer pitches, at a cost of $40m. The restaurant itself cost a mere $4.5m.

. . .

  Worse, it has taken McDonald's 14 years of relentless effort to open its first restaurant. In 1976 the company began talks aimed at opening a restaurant at the 1980 Olympic Games in Moscow. That prospect died when western countries boycotted the games after the Soviet Union's invasion of Afghanistan. McDonald's hopes only managed to survive by a fluke; the Moscow McDonald's is being operated not by the American parent but by its Canadian subsidiary. When the deal died in 1980, the Soviet ambassador in Canada was Mr Alexander Yakovlev, a would-be reformer whom Leonid Brezhnev had dispatched into diplomatic exile. Mr Yakovlev told Mr George Cohon, the head of the Canadian operation: "Don't lose heart. At the moment this is ideologically impossible. One day you will be able to do it." Today Mr Yakovlev, a sidekick of Mr Mikhail Gorbachev, is one of the most influential figures in the Soviet Union.

  Restarted in earnest after Russia's first joint-venture law in 1987, negotiations for this one $50m deal have taken about half of Mr Cohon's time, a huge commitment for a man running a $1 billion-a-year business. If Soviet leaders think that other chief executives can spend this amount of time on a single deal, they will be sorely disappointed.

(*The Economist*, 3–9 February 1990)

Benetton

Nominating a business which started as a family group of four in 1965 and which entered the eighties relatively unknown outside Italy as a world class brand may seem premature. However, dollar for dollar, I wonder whether any branding has ever identified a more promising promotional message than Benetton. Although Benetton still has some way to go before it can be compared with such branding superpowers as Coca-Cola and McDonald's, it has passed triumphantly through a world class brand's formative stages.

A brand which is set up to market fashion's newest colours sounds like an ambitious enterprise. The majority of long-life fashion marques have relied on an accumulation of snob values. In a sense these brands succeed by becoming powerful enough to dictate their own lines on how to be 'in fashion'. Benetton consciously opted for a different route – a brand designed to be the consumers' mirror to changing fashions at street level.

To symbolize this, Benetton chose to home in on the common ingredient of all fashions – colours. Around this theme it has been building a solar system of mental images. The original meaning of 'the United Colours of Benetton' appeared to be an invitation to consumers to join the brand in making the world a more colourful place. Benetton's wardrobe appeared to be far more liberated in its sense of colour than the *haute couturists*.

Quite soon, the United Colours of Benetton took on an additional cultural meaning. Colours became connected with voting for multiracial harmony. Its advertising clearly communicated that Benetton's clan comprised members of every race. Benetton's communication of this theme seemed to be born with a natural fluency. Women's magazines would carry Benetton snapshots looking like a collegiate photograph of the class of '82, with the difference that the class was highly colourful both in its choice of Benetton attire and in its composition of varied racial hues. As Benetton's rapport with its public grew, more poignant celebrations of the theme have been employed, like the photo of a black mother breastfeeding her white baby.

Throughout the brand's progression, the simultaneous translations of 'the United Colours of Benetton' have grown more numerous in its shops. A visit to a Benetton shop is quite likely to introduce you to a dozen languages or more.

Benetton does not like to use the word 'franchise' in connection with its thousands of retailers. It explains their independence like this:

> Each shop is granted free use of the (Benetton) label on the under-
> standing that it will adopt a Benetton style of decor and only sell
> Benetton products ordered through the representative. The com-
> pany's representatives are appointed to note consumer trends,
> promote Benetton products, assist local entrepreneurs to open
> new shops, monitor client operations and purchase a complete
> collection of Benetton garments for marketing.

This pseudo-franchising works to maximum effect. Benetton
shops always manage a sparkling layout – a visual treat for shoppers that represents a thoroughly harmonious combination of a
trader's self-ownership and a carefully planned branding framework. Benetton increasingly revels in using the best international shopping locations as a significant part of its own media
coverage: the brand's colourful showcases are a natural fixture
wherever both tourists and locals like to mingle.

Benetton's world of colours is also branching outside its
franchise system in carefully selected ways. For example, its
'Colours' range of perfumes is designed to be on display in department stores. The packaging not only befits a product with a
smart message, but also serves as another flagship of Benetton's
universal appeal.

In another venture, which aims to increase the visibility of its
children's clothes, Benetton is teaming up with Mattel, the
maker of Barbie dolls. We may all soon be looking to 'the United
Colours of Benetton's Barbies' to show off the latest fashions in
toyworld.

Unlike McDonald's, which set about developing a new product
category, Benetton carved out its original business from a mature
marketplace. Its marketing mix looks like a new generation of
brand which many world class prototypes may follow.

Interestingly, *The Economist* appears to be as optimistic about
Benetton as a model of manufacturing versatility in a converging
marketplace as I am about the brand's organized consumer
identity:

> To the impatient, cross-border mergers look the swiftest way to
> grow across Europe – and seem the surest route to market power
> if they snare well-known brands as well. Brides and bridegrooms
> get instant access to foreign suppliers, factories, sales-and-
> marketing networks and often cheaper labour. Some of Europe's

Benetton's multiracial harmony.

smaller carmakers have decided that the only way to survive the spiralling costs of product development is to team up with a sugar daddy. So Miss Jaguar married Ford, and Miss Saab is living with GM.

Such mergers can be messy. Cross-border acquisitions may take up to three times longer to complete than domestic ones, thanks to accounting complications. Once they are completed, the most talented local managers often depart through revolving doors. The newest technologies (flexible manufacturing, faster computers and better telecommunications) have reduced the optimum size of many businesses. The odds are that they will reduce it even more. . . .

In short, the route to pan-European efficiency in what is done centrally may be quite different to the best strategy for building market-share where the actual sales are made. Benetton, an Italian clothing company, shows how to serve a big but variegated market. Behind Benetton's shops lies a computer-controlled network of flexible factories, warehouses and suppliers: a high-tech hub-and-spoke network. When local fashions change, Benetton's manufacturing centre can respond in a trice.

The company's network allows it to act local while reaping the benefits of being transnational. Megamerged Euro-conglomerates – riveted together, lock stock and barrel – may find that rather harder.

Branded Stage Management

Purchases are made to be consumed and witnessed. I make no apologies for repeating this sentence often, because every time you apply it to a brand you may key into a fresh insight – another slice of life – for the brand's rationale in its consumers' world.

If consumers are to perceive a brand as more than a naked product, the 'more' must be the added character which brings a brand to life. The characteristics which we associate with things as well as people embrace the full spectrum of emotional bonds which we feel and experience. On what sorts of axes do the bonds of relationships take shape? Attraction and repulsion? Competing and sharing? Safe and dangerous? Serious and humorous? Child and adult? Male and female? Super-efficient and gently sensitive? Crowded and lonely? Self-deception and self-doubt? Enumerating these lifelines individually often seems to be an artificial exercise, but this is only to say that human lifestyles are a whole play of changing scenes, not an actor's momentary lines. For example, the brand of drink which I would like to be seen with when I am out with the lads is different from the brand I choose when I have a night out with my girlfriend, and is different from the brand I drink alone at home.

Far from being intangibles, the bonds of branding create quite concrete realities. We see repeated evidence for this in every consumer who is prepared to pay more for a Coca-Cola than a local brand of cola, even when he or she cannot distinguish which is which in a tasting where the brands' identities are hidden. The key to the bonds of branding is to explore product–people interrelationships in every way that they emerge from the eternal triangle of consumer marketing:

Who purchases? – Who consumes? – Who witnesses?
. . . where? when? with whom? why? . . .

The social theatres associated with product categories revolve round different kinds of triangular affairs. Figure 3.1 shows some examples.

As brands become the most visible props of everyday human dramas, they talk for the products which they represent with in-built emotional scripts. Crowd-pullers include the images that individuals want to wear to impress their peers; the touches of empathy which prove to be private morale-builders; the aids to the burdens of 'gatekeeping' for a family, ranging from the maternal pressure to select safe products for infants, to the frustrations of the under-appreciated provider; the assistant that helps to take the double-guessing out of finding a gift which a friend will appreciate.

An eye for the nuances of social interaction involved in the usage of a particular product category helps us to diagnose how emotional bonds are branded. Why do so many detergent brands continue to campaign so pointedly on whiteness now that almost all of today's wash in coloured? The sociological answer is that whiteness is the key symbol for communicating to the housewife's pride that her family will be seen by neighbours and peers to have the best-turned-out clothes. Compare this with a campaign on biological stain removal. The emotional ground has shifted completely. The brand is no longer appealing to a visible expression of family pride, but is now intimating a feeling of superior skill associated with a home scientist who knows how to choose the most efficient product to do the job.

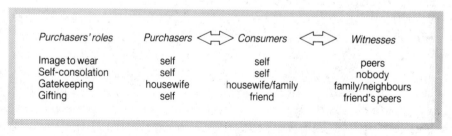

Purchasers' roles	Purchasers	Consumers	Witnesses
Image to wear	self	self	peers
Self-consolation	self	self	nobody
Gatekeeping	housewife	housewife/family	family/neighbours
Gifting	self	friend	friend's peers

Figure 3.1 Examples of social theatres for branded products.

Social features

One of the impacts of modern technology on many consumer-goods categories is that manufacturers can no longer bank on new product features for very long before competitors catch up. These days, the communications battle between established brands is not concerned solely with being the first to boast an extra product feature. The important thing is to be the first to present the feature in a way that adds significance to your brand. The new feature will then take on a symbolic justification in the marketplace which supports your brand and detracts from competitors. For example, when the gel form of toothpaste became a fashionable addition in the eighties, largely assured by its colourful impact on the television screen, it was quite astonishing to see how different brands around the world were the first to justify gel in their national images. In one country gel's justification bolstered a brand's tradition of extra freshness; in another country gel was justified parentally as making teeth-brushing fun for your children; elsewhere gel was successfully presented as the ultra-medicinal product form.

In this way gel's colourful message took on varied social implications around the world. A moral for branders is that it is never too early to start considering the way that any new features in the R & D pipeline may be put up for social adoption in the marketplace. If, for example, laundry detergents become five times more concentrated in the nineties, ask yourself which established brand has the most to gain: 'the family pride' (whiteness and safeness); 'the master-of-science' (efficient biological stain removal); the 'friends of the green' or the 'post-housewife' (showy and modern in its packaging, liberated in its portrayal of household responsibilities).

Branding's in-built script

At any stage of brand development, one of the best pieces of research a brander can do is on him- or herself or on other marketing colleagues. For example, what are some of the self-consoling reasons for buying a brand as a deliberate act of private consumption? A treat for me, an interruption from boredom, an aid to concentration, a change of mood, a reassuring habit, a vote of faith, a souvenir of good times . . . such lists are never finished. Every time you make one, you may find a better phrase for encapsulating a human cause. We can start to record many of these emotional reactions as stage directions which have a common meaning in the universal play of consumerism. So the next time you meet someone who doubts the possibilities of global branding, begin with the question: is he/she thinking of branding the right things?

Today, the profitable heartland of branded communications often lies in the emotional experiences on offer rather than the direct comparisons of product functions. This is not to belittle the importance of product excellence, but the world class brand should be concerned with permanence and universality since the newsworthiness of particular product benefits may come and go.

If your brand is to perform in a global theatre, the script you broadcast should be mainly concerned with developing emotional associations, connections of relevance and long-term effects.

Temporary product functions and lines geared to instant local applause are subsidiary to a wider structural mission, an enduring sense of character. Shakespeare knew how to create immortal characters. Is it unrealistic to expect that world class branders should apply a similar knowhow to their craft? After all, they are creating character scripts involving millions of consumer rehearsals every day. And the budgets spent on staging these brands are more lavish than Shakespeare could ever have dreamed of, then or now. Returning to Chapter Two's example of McDonald's contribution to the Moscow scene, is this not the kind of heroic act of corporate character which associates McDonald's with a universal feeling of goodwill?

Purchasers–consumers–witnesses is a global construct, but its value to a scriptwriter depends on an eye for local details. Branding's worldly touch percolates a feeling of global participation through individually human, and apparently private, acts of consumption. In this profile of the impact of brand leaders on a British household, courtesy of *Marketing* magazine, the count of global brands currently equals that of local ones. (What odds would you give in a rematch in a decade's time?)

It is Monday morning. Bleary eyed and miserable, he struggles to put on his Persil-washed clothes and thinks to himself, "I must have a cup of Nescafé". Steaming mug of coffee in his hand, he dunks a bag of PG Tips into a cup for her. Thoughts turn to breakfast; Kellogg's Corn Flakes followed by toast spread with Flora. And seeing as it's Monday, some Heinz Baked Beans, and another cup of Nescafé.

Look at the time. He quickly douses the dishes in some Fairy Liquid, gives the cat its Whiskas, and the dog its Pedigree Chum, while she changes the baby's Pampers (where are those new moist baby wipes?). She stuffs some Heinz baby food down baby, while husband's off to the toilet. Damn! Where's the Andrex? Rush to the bathroom, a quick brush with Colgate toothpaste and a frantic dash down stairs and into the waiting Ford Sierra.

For elevenses it's a Kit-Kat and a can of Coke. For lunch a Big Mac. Back home before dinner, a quick can of Carlsberg Special for him and a snifter of Gordon's for her. Something quick and easy for dinner? How about pasta? "We can open a jar of Dolmio sauce." Baby to bed, dinner over, slump into the settee and relax with a shot of Bell's.

Even a decade ago, this little cameo would have been unthinkable. Branding was only just coming of age and many of these brands did not exist. It is a testimony to the power of brands that today, unlike any other period in human history, we automatically think in terms of brands to cater for our needs and desires. A profile of the brand buying habits of the British public comes close to a study of its way of life.

Borrowing from the history of advertising, three creeds for a brand's sense of purpose receive most prominence wherever marketing is taught. As we review these, it is worth keeping purchasers–consumers–witnesses in mind. The aim will be to turn each creed into a question for world class branders to ponder.

The unique selling point

Rosser Reeves originally defined the Unique Selling Point (USP) as the three-in-one purpose of effective advertising:

(1) Each advertisement must make a proposition to the consumer. Not just words, not just product puffery, not just show-window advertising. Each advertisement must say to each reader: "Buy this product, and you will get this specific benefit".

(2) The proposition must be one that the competition either cannot, or does not, offer. It must be unique – either a uniqueness of the brand or a claim not otherwise made in that particular field of advertising.

(3) The proposition must be so strong that it can move the mass millions, i.e., pull over new customers to your product.

When we look at this definition, we should keep in mind that it exemplified Reeves' philosophy for effective advertising in the USA between 1930 and 1960. Thirty years on we can afford to make a sub-editor's suggestion for a change to the last line of Reeves' first clause: 'Buy this brand and you will participate in this particular experience'.

Every brander owes a particular debt to Reeves. He compiled the empirical evidence which shows why a unique point of distinction should be the core of every brand. The brand which establishes a distinctive position tends to pre-empt this in consumers' minds. Provided a brand projects its original position consistently, it is seldom cost-effective for another brand to try challenging it head-on. The reason, which Reeves demonstrated, is that consumers loyal to the original brand tend to see the challenger as a usurper to their trusted brand's throne. So the nature of branding is a double-edged sword. A brand with an original position pre-empts its own unique credentials. But as a brand is a long-term investment, a position should be created in a style which allows the business to evolve and expand over time.

First question of world class branding

Why invest in the enormous commitment of a world class brand unless there is a worldly USP to build on?

The image

Martin Meyer in his vintage history of advertising (*Madison Avenue USA*) dubbed David Ogilvy as 'the apostle of the brand image'. In today's marketing jargon, image refers to all the ways that branding reflects on the perceptions of a product or company, but in Meyer's original terminology of the fifties the image school of advertising focused on the power of the brand as a visible status symbol.

For decades, all new employees at the advertising agency Ogilvy & Mather would receive a booklet of Ogilvy's indoctrinations which included: 'It pays to give your brand a first-class ticket through life. People don't like to be seen consuming products which their friends regard as third-class'.

If anything, this understates the case in favour of a cultivated visibility. A brand which is consistently seen to have the right credentials commutes its way upwards through all the environments of branding. Upwards through 'consumer spirals' of purchasers ↔ consumers ↔ witnesses, where the witness who is impressed by consumption in turn becomes the consumer who impresses other witnesses. Upwards through the corporate environment of shareholders ↔ employees ↔ customers ↔ trade ↔ journalists ↔ society ↔ governments to the extent that governments may even compete to be a host country for the brand's corporate centres. Transnationally, as an entry in the global dictionary of the best. (We will return to a detailed discussion of 'the environments of branding' in Chapter Five.)

Second question of world class branding

Does the brand have sufficient status and forums of visibility to encourage ever-growing circles of people to elect the brand as an international symbol of excellence?

Empathy

Brand empathy is about the process of developing human rapport which advances along the personal touchline from a feeling of 'this brand understands me' to a feeling of 'this brand is me'. Sometimes the process goes a step further to a feeling of 'this brand shows me that other people are like me'. Before we get misty-eyed about the process, let us look at a case history. Here is an extract from Julian Lewis Watkins' fifties' testimony to Betty Crocker – a branding which has held its own communion with American housewives for most of this century:

> Of all corporate symbols, Betty Crocker is probably the best known among women. A recent survey among housewives showed that 99% of the women of America recognise her as a sort of "First Lady of Food", the most highly esteemed home service authority in the nation and a real friend to millions of women.
>
> James A. Quint, Advertising Manager was responsible for the first use of the name "Betty Crocker" in correspondence in November 1921. But before that, was a long-practiced belief on the part of management in the philosophy and doctrine of sincere, helpful home service, and that this service should be personalised and feminised.
>
> A community of spirit between the home-maker and manufacturer is a simple idea, but it takes a special kind of genius to recognise its importance, and make it work.
>
> . . .
>
> Several agencies and many people have played important parts in continuing and building the 'personalised, feminised' scope of Betty Crocker service, but in my book I happen to like "all the rest

of your natural life" – an ad which made just about the highest pre-test ratings in 30 years of General Mills operation. Read Jean Rindlaub's copy and you will see why:

> All the rest of your natural life
> The first birthday. And the first step. And the first word. And the first day of school. And the first mumps. And the first bumps too big to kiss away. And the first date and the first dance and the first roses and the first love and the joys and terrors and triumphs of the days that lie between. They are all here . . . in a single moment, in a single family, lost in the wonder of the first baby . . . and this first birthday.
>
>   Don't go away. It's a moment to remember. A moment to mark with a very special cake . . . one that's nothing less than perfect. A cake you just know must be made from Betty Crocker Cake Mix. . . .

Such was the pinnacle of print advertising of yesteryear, whereas today's advertisers build brands with the higher empathy-grabbing medium of television. However, the fundamentals of empathy branding remain unchanged, that is, to establish a communion between brand and consumer which is quite personal in its appeal to the imagination, even though the heart of the matter is orchestrated to be a consistent bestseller.

  Incidentally, as the indomitable spirit of the middle-western

Portraying Betty Crocker across generations.

housewife, Betty Crocker is alive and well in America today representing over 100 product lines. Recently her seventh portrait was formally painted. Betty's age, you see, never changes, her attire shows modest changes with the times but is always corporate red with a little while embroidery below the neck, her eyes follow over you like Mona Lisa's but with the essential difference that hers twinkle with homely care.

Third question of world class branding

Does the brand promote an experience of belonging by reaching out to the most personal areas of the human imagination with such confidence and familiarity that it feels like a kindred spirit?

Drawing on our discussion of advertising creeds, Figure 3.2 confirms a second three-in-one structure for brands to exploit. Many world class brands aim to perpetrate a high awareness of all three answers to the question: who is special?

Among the founding fathers of advertising, I reserve pride of place for the wisdom of James Webb Young documented in his book *How to Become an Advertising Man*. Although Young finished practising almost half a century ago, I cannot think of a better test of an advertising campaign than that of asking which, if any, of Young's statements of social intent are incorporated in the script:

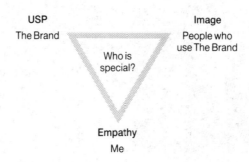

Figure 3.2 Branding's emotive trinity.

'We can discover, I think, that there are five basic ways advertising works. These are:

(1) By familiarising, that is, as the dictionary says by "making something well-known; bringing into common use". We will see that this is the absolutely basic value created by advertising, the one underlying all others.
(2) By reminding – a function that may alone, in some cases, make advertising pay.
(3) By spreading news, not only news in the newspaper sense, but a special kind of news that only advertising, in the commercial way, can most widely deal with.
(4) By overcoming inertias – the great drag on all human progress, economic or non-economic, as represented in the sociological term "cultural lag".
(5) By adding a value not in the product – the most challenging field for creativeness in advertising.'

Uniting The World's Marketplaces

Megapositions

Historically, many brands were planned rather like arranged marriages. Products were there, images needed to be found. Advertising experts would search locally for images which best fit each of a company's products. Recently, an increasing number of global marketers have had the cheek to ask a heretic's question. In developing a global brand which should come first: the product or an image which the brand can develop into a pre-emptive consumer experience worldwide?

Many of the brands which achieved global status during the eighties seemed image-led, by design. Foster's was introduced around the world as the spirit of the Australian male; Benetton issued the invitation to join the brand's club and make the world a more colourful place; Timotei offered nature's mildness.

We can argue whether such megapositioning styles are a limited resource. They should epitomize a universal consumer rationale such as friendliness, a royal sense of taste, parenthood or natural goodness. They must also connote this in a way which is readily transferable across national boundaries thereby gaining quick recognition and uniform understanding. Often, we may feel that a successful spiritual design could be defining a merchandiser's sense of style, or a corporate rationale for excellence, as much as a reason for manufacturing one isolated type of product.

CEOs who now pay fancy prices for the goodwill of famous

brands are also prioritizing their companies' investments in megapositioning images. The reorganizational implications are subtle. An identity of worldwide repute presents a leading position in the race for world marketplaces and offers considerable rewards, but can its new owner cultivate it assiduously?

Images, being nebulous things, have often been undervalued in business accounting. Concrete investments like new factories have also been a lot easier for CEOs to show off to their shareholders. Since the late eighties, the pendulum has started to swing the other way. Brands have gained belated interest among the financial community to the extent that the goodwill futures of many brands are now overrated. Other brands remain seriously undervalued, particularly where businesses have yet to fully recognize themselves as brands.

Harrods is a prime example. Its previous owners seriously underestimated the business worth by thinking of Harrods merely as an exotic store, as did Britain's Department of Trade and Industry in supervising takeover protocols. Most Europeans identify this merchandiser's credentials as epitomizing almost royal taste. Even in France, not normally a nation lacking in its own senses of style, department stores compete over such slogans as 'The Harrods of Paris'. Yet Harrods began the nineties with one European outlet, in Knightsbridge, unless you count a delicatessen counter in the duty-free section of Frankfurt airport. The store's expert taste is likely to prove one of the biggest licensing opportunities of the decade.

When an excellent local service integrates image and product in a transportable way, it may also be ripe for megapositioning. McDonald's and Kentucky Fried Chicken spent several decades as local American diners proving the demand for, and improving the streamlining of, their offer. Both were almost accidentally discovered as prototype global brands by the individuals who promoted them as world class franchises.

More brands will be discovered as having world class potential through two business developments. First, companies need to become more organizationally aware of the total business impact of franchising and image-led branding. Second, a shorthand valuation system, summarizing key aspects of a brand's future potential, is needed so that managers sharing in the coordination of a brand's growth around the world have a higher common understanding of its asset value. Business functions have become so compartmentalized that marketers, while drowning in data about their brand, often do not even know its actual profitability to the firm.

Brand organizations

Branders who intend to organize businesses around world class images will need to be inquisitive, asking questions like these:

- Which positioning experiences offer the greatest international scope for building on?
- Which of these positions matches a range of products in our portfolio?
- What existing globally recognized identities 'talk the same language' as the image which we wish to own?
- Have we the commitment to this image, financially and personally, to make it our business to be the first to come to mind in this way among audiences around the world?

Consider an image war in which the world's most popular brand represents products 'designed for men that women like'. Those racing to pre-empt this position would be dealing firstly in intangible properties and only secondly in physical products. Even a brand as large as Marlboro, which owns this position in cigarettes, may not have the clout – as a single product – to compete as the world's number one in, say, menswear. So world class branding strategies will increasingly depend on the evolution of two kinds of business practice:

(1) Conglomerates will organize their world class brands across products with similar images, resulting in a matrix structure of operating subsidiaries (product sources) and branded subsidiaries (image sources).
(2) Everyone, should explore franchising and licensing opportunities.

Anti-smoking trends may mean that Philip Morris has left it too late to extend Marlboro's core business. Indeed, Gillette's recent renaissance focuses on its strategic intent to take over the mantle of the clean-shaven-hero brand – an image which is being led by its pan-American and pan-European campaign 'The Best A Man Can Get'.

Other conglomerates may have little time to commit themselves to images which would make worthy subsidiaries in a world of transnationally organized businesses. Consider Unilever. If this company decided to transform Timotei's promise of natural mildness into a subsidiary company, here are some of the marketing steps which Timotei Inc. might take:

- Acquire The Body Shop and rename it Timotei's Body Shop.
- Develop recognition of a green globe logo around Timotei's name both for corporate use and to identify products licensed under Timotei's image.
- Sponsor a world prize for the best 'green' paper providing a balanced understanding between 'green needs' and global prosperity.
- Develop 'green' holidays. Start by putting the Timotei name on countryside hotels of excellence, and progress to joint ventures with Disney to build themeparks focusing on the wonders of the natural world.

You may enjoy thinking of better ways of commercializing the spirit of this 'green' positioning, but we can already predict that many world class brands will pre-empt homely virtues by being those most visibly committed to a globally common sense.

The opportunity of a world class image is to develop a business exchange between customers and employees connected by a shared concern for the values and standards which the image evokes.

Marketing soap is a competitive business. In its day, Lux, the brand of film stars, was the most original imagery for branding soap. In parts of the world, that day lives on where soap bars are the main manufactured cosmetic that women can afford for facial cleansing. However, in many developed countries, the image has outgrown the product. Ms Average, not just film stars, spends lots of money on other kinds of skin-care products designed specifically for the face. Everyday soaps are also out-shone for glamour by *haute couture* rivals.

Even if Levers view Lux as a brand that has a first duty to market soap, extraordinarily few non-soap lines have been allowed to evolve from Lux's long-established global image. If Lux had been its own corporate subsidiary, the *bon mot* of one Lux brand manager might have had some substance: 'Perhaps these days we should allow studios to use our brand's communication vehicle to create new film stars'.

Though the principle of promoting a brand to become a company is not new, precedents have usually taken place at times of corporate crisis. Witness the transformation of British Leyland (or BL as it anonymously called itself in its latter days) into Rover Group and Jaguar cars. In the future, some of the biggest corporate opportunities will come from planned promotions of brands into corporate subsidiaries. Just as product unbundling has been found to give conglomerates a renewed focus, so will image unbundling.

For a vision of the freedom that corporate brands have to make the most of themselves, think of Disney's progression as a company which has always enjoyed living with its image. While Walt may never have imagined that his cartoons would grow up in our mass-communications age to be the world's number one branding of the magic of childhood, few marketers today can imagine any other brand challenging Disney for this global crown. The company takes great care to ensure that the Disney spirit is handed on through generations of employees, as is evident from the policy that all staff, from top executives downwards, should serve annual stints in the themeparks. The reward is a brand that other businesses and governments queue up to work with.

Here is *Euromarketing's* summary report of the reasons why Disney will have over $100 million of meaning to Nestlé over the next decade:

(*Euromarketing*, 16 January 1990)

> *Nestlé to focus on Disney promotions during the next decade*
> – following a licensing agreement with Walt Disney Consumer Products signed in Paris last week. Sources at Nestlé headquarters in Vevey, Switzerland, say the deal is likely to mean that the

Sunday in the park with Disney.

world's largest food company will begin pouring large sums into in-store and other promotions while maintaining regular media budgets. . . . The licensing agreement represents a major coup for Nestlé. Under the deal, Nestlé will be the only food company allowed to use Disney characters and properties in promotions in Western and Eastern Europe, the USSR, the Middle East and North Africa. Nestlé will pay Walt Disney Consumer Products a percentage of trade sales of all food items sold in conjunction with Disney characters until the year 2002. Nestlé plans an array of new product introductions related to Disney characters.

- Nestlé expects to have paid Disney around $176 million for the connection when the renewable contract expires.

- The Disney program will be the focus of Nestlé's marketing activities in Europe for the next decade. "Instead of having a thousand new ideas, you can concentrate on just one" says Michael Reinarz, Nestlé's director of visual communications in Vevey. "It's perfect."

- A key attraction of the deal is that Nestlé can now approach major retail operations in Europe with an unbeatable proposition: in-store Disney promotions for Nestlé products which will build customer traffic. Mr Reinarz has been searching for a communications program for Nestlé which is more efficient than media advertising. This is it.

- Nestlé's Mickey Mousse chocolate-flavoured dessert, introduced in West Germany three years ago, is a big success for the company. The product features Disney's Mickey Mouse on the packaging, but is not supported by advertising. Sales are phenomenal – $6 million annually.

The opposite pole to the corporate brand is evident when companies choose new brand names for every new product – a multibranding strategy which until recently was advocated by such leading branders as Procter & Gamble. As a result the images owned become as fragmented as the communications budgets.

The seventies were the heyday of brand fragmentation. American authors Trout and Ries in their bestselling book on positioning inspired Western marketers – with coverage of their precision ideology in an ensuing generation of marketing textbooks – to direct a single-tracked attack on their prospects' minds. Product positionings should be separately identified 'like DieHard for a longer-lasting battery or Shake 'N' Bake for a new way to cook chicken'. Line extending was categorized as a 'sickness' which could only dilute a brand's franchise by diluting the focal characteristics of the original product.

It was difficult for brand managers to confront Trout and Ries's thesis because most of the logic was right as far as it went. It is a compelling idea to think of a brand's *raison d'être* as that of a competitive agent targeting communications with the aim of being seen by people as the number one (in something even if you define what that something is).

In branding, being seen to own number one position is not merely about enjoying the winner's spoils. It usually pre-empts competitors from challenging you head-on. As we noted in the previous chapter, Rosser Reeves demonstrated over 40 years ago that the commercial advantage of a brand's unique selling point is that loyal consumers tend to dismiss an imitative new brand as a rude pretender to the leader's throne. The success of market segmentation strategies depend on this principle.

By the late seventies, targeting had reached the stage where many Western brand managers were developing new brands to identify the smallest of unique product niches. Taking the logic to an extreme point, large multinational companies were seriously considering branding a single line such as the cheapest substitute chicken which you could roast in your oven. This was never likely to be a proper use of the advertising budget (where will such a brand lead to long term?) or of their overheads (how many marginal brands does a mature manufacturing company want to administer?). These were the days when nine out of ten new brands failed because companies were going through the exercise of new product development, in spite of computer predictions that the market was so crowded that strongly executed targeting with a new brand would fill a gap representing half the sales the company's accountants set.

In retrospect, we can see that disciples of the Trout–Ries positioning school were often targeting branded identities at a level which was too detailed, too product-dependent and too local. To avoid the trap of the microbrand, megapositioning is practised by asking: what is the broadest level at which we can brand a number one business?

Not every company can be a Disney, so let us apply a thought experiment to the kind of household products marketed by Procter & Gamble. What lifestyles or mindsets interact with a range of household chores? Could we brand a range of products to relate to one of these human senses of purpose? The clues are there in many leading household brands, but surprisingly many of these potent image-leaders remain today as isolated representatives of a single product category.

Putting the pieces together, here are some examples of potential house-leading images. The *parental brand* which is the clear leader among traditional mums who like to use the brand which is recommended (and is most widely acknowledged by peers) as producing the best (or safest) results for all the family. The *master-of-science* brand which is strong and scientifically efficient so that you feel you are managing the task in the most expert way. The *post-housewife* brand which is modern and showy. This brand relates to singles of both sexes as well as *liberated* households by adding a high profile to the job and suggesting that the job-doer should never be taken for granted.

Casting aside the fuzziness of my stereotyping, we can debate whether multibranders really want (say) 10 different parental brands to represent their products in 10 different household categories. As late as 1987 Procter & Gamble's CEO John Smale reorganized his company's internally competing brand managers under a matrix of general managers, noting caustically that 'the historical way of managing Procter & Gamble no longer fits well the company that we are today, nor the business environment in which we must compete'.

Interesting local examples of extendible P & G brands have now started to sprout. One is the Fairy brand in the UK, whose heritage as a mild and gentle product is principally due to its historical dominance of the dishwash liquid market. This product category gives Fairy its own window of visibility alongside most of Britain's kitchen sinks. Capitalizing on this awareness, the Fairy range now includes laundry detergents and toilet soaps all united by a house symbol of a striding infant. Unlike other baby motifs, Fairy's badge has been designed with such simplicity that it can be reproduced at thumbnail size (for example, for an imprint on a soap bar or as punctuation marks in printed slogans) as well as in larger sizes for packaging impact.

We may expect to see the striding infant symbol communicating across many national frontiers on Procter & Gamble's milder products for 'parental' households. I would not be surprised if this commercial identity eventually achieves as broad recognition around the world as Lacoste's brilliantly designed alligator. In P & G's jungle, like that of many Western conglomerates, world class marketing will involve rationalization of a lot of branding identities.

Valuation of branded futures – a management shorthand

Faced with the prospect of converging markets, managers of transnational companies will increasingly need to decide which of their branded identities to promote to transnational status, and which to retain as local communication vehicles. Similarly, those who are developing new brands, or acquiring or forming an alliance with others will need to be clear about the transnational appeal of the images with which they are electing to run. I would suggest that comparisons of the future credential brands should begin by rating three aspects of their marketability:

(1) Is the brand designed as *world class* or local?

In integrating with a global society, the relationships which a world class identity develops with its customers are only one important side of the coin; the brand must also ensure that it does not offend other audiences who will judge it, such as shareholders, traders, journalists, pressure groups and governments. Has the brand made sufficient strategic alliances in each of the three transnational megamarkets of Europe (West and East), the Americas (North and South) and Japan (and rising suns) to avoid any protectionism against foreigners?

(2) How strong are the opportunities to *expand* the brand's businesses in the next five years?

Expansion of business may come from the growth of existing markets or extensions into new countries or new product categories. The choice of a five year time-span for envisaging what a brand may next achieve is somewhat arbitrary, but has the advantage of corresponding to the maximum period of a secondary 'futures budget' which Peter Drucker (*The Economist*, 21 October 1989) advocates to CEOs 'to cover the work needed to build and maintain the company's wealth producing capacity'.

(3) How strong is the brand's *marketing edge as a defence* against possible risks?

A complete audit of risks should be considered: for example, product risks include a 'quantum leap' in competitor's technology; channel risks include fundamental changes in distributive, media or regulatory forces acting on the marketplace; image risks include a weakly pre-emptive image or one which clashes with socio–environmental trends. As as investment of goodwill in a single entity the brand can be an vulnerable as its weakest organizational link.

Brand valuation systems should focus on simple toplines of this sort, so that management can easily make adjustments for alternative competitive and environmental scenarios across the company's portfolio of brands. Figure 4.1 itemizes an ABC rating

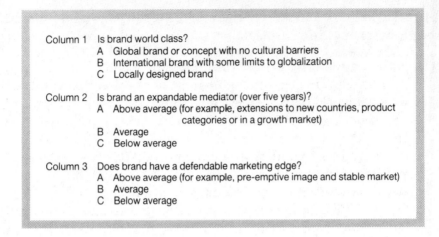

Figure 4.1 Brand valuation: ABC ratings system.

system, based on the three aspects of marketability described above, for contrasting the future credentials of brands. Let us turn to some examples, since the process of discussing a brand's rating should guide managers to a directional consensus on its future as an organizational investment.

AAA EXAMPLES OF EXPANDING WORLD CLASS BRANDS

Disney, Hilton, Sony, Lacoste, Benetton . . . from a cast of thousands, I mention these five brands because of their variety of images. With luck, every reader of this book in the 1990s will rate these brands as (1) globally welcome, (2) fast-expanding businesses partly because of the added-value images which they have built and (3) owning megapositions which it would not be cost-effective for competitors to attack directly.

Some of these brands are a medium in their own right. They do not have to rely on the commercial break to grow their images. All of them have showcase products, and settings which control the standards against which consumers judge the competition.

Disney's medium originated with cartoons. The Hilton's medium is the international tourist's guidebook where it sets the yardstick for de luxe hotels. Sony's role is to bring the mass media to you with the quiet confidence of the brand which announces itself with the product sticker 'it's a Sony'.

Lacoste owns one of the world's most successful trademarks pitched on probably the most impactful advertising hoarding – namely, people's breasts. Benetton's trading medium was reviewed in Chapter Two.

None of these AAA brands think of themselves as a single product. They have tended to think of themselves as clubs of excellence and have grabbed every opportunity to project lifestyles and social experiences which members (in other words, customers) enjoy. Disneyland is for warming family experiences, Hilton space is for the feeling of exclusivity, the Sony universe is science as a state-of-the-art form, the Lacoste exchange is an adult sense of humour and the Benetton community is multiracial freedom of spirit.

Watch these spaces because each may have the power to endorse a yet untold number of products in its own image.

> The opening of a retail store in central London this Saturday selling cartoon videos, Christmas gifts, and cuddly toys might normally attract little attention in the run-up to Christmas.
>
> Apart from being opened by Mickey Mouse himself, not only is the store the first of the Walt Disney company's scheduled European retail ventures but it is also larger than most of the 75 Disney stores already operating in the US. So the razzmatazz surrounding the opening is understandable.
>
> Walt Disney World in Florida is the most popular single overseas destination for British package holiday-makers after Majorca in Spain, so the Mouse is enormously popular with Britons. Yet the store is not an isolated attempt to cash in on the Mouse's familiarity; rather it is the tip of a carefully co-ordinated cross-marketing campaign intended to fully exploit the Disney brand name and maximise its profit potential worldwide.
>
> "We have a clear goal that every part of the Disney operation should not only make money but should also be used to support each other as much as possible," explains Jack Meyers, Walt Disney's vice-president in charge of international marketing.
>
> The three Disney areas of operation are the theme park attractions (in Los Angeles, Orlando, Tokyo and soon Paris); the film studios (it is now Hollywood's number one production company); and consumer products, ranging from everything from videos to

collectors' items such as film "cels" – individually painted celluloid film stills – from Disney's animated movies.

Capturing the loyalty of children is obviously vital to Disney's future both in the short term for sales of cartoon videos and cuddly toys and also with the longer-term aim of repeat visits to the theme parks for them and their children.

Disney has negotiated with television stations in nine European countries to air a regular Disney Club show. "The Disney Clubs are an important part of keeping our target market in Europe aware of what is happening at Euro Disney" confirms Jean-Marie Gerbeaux, Euro Disneyland's marketing vice president. He acknowledges that this was precisely the technique pioneered by Walt Disney himself when progress at the Disneyland theme park under construction was shown on the weekly Walt Disney Show in the 1950s.

Disney was also one of the pioneers of successful cross-marketing from television to shops, a technique which is now standard marketing practice. The legend of Davy Crockett, fighter of Red Indians, was well and truly established in American folklore through the television show Disney produced (at a loss) in the mid-1950s; but the sale under licence of coonskin hats as worn by Davy Crockett and the number one hit in the US, The Ballad of Davy Crockett, earned the company substantial profits and turned the show into a financial success.

Disney is currently choosing an agency in a four-way pitch to mastermind its advertising campaign for Euro Disneyland. Most of this advertising – at least in the near future – is to be aimed at the trade rather than the consumer. This approach emphasises that Disney's marketing is not always directly targeted at the consumer. Next month, for example, its roadshow takes off across the continent of Europe to tell travel agents about developments at Disney both in the US and Paris.

(*The Financial Times*, Thursday 1 November 1990)

ABA EXAMPLES OF MATURE WORLD CLASS BRANDS

Levi's, Head & Shoulders . . . these are examples of mature world class businesses with strongly defined branded territories which should not be overextended by an attempt to use the brand to endorse completely new kinds of products.

In the early eighties, Levi's experimented with several non-denim ranges. They met with mixed success. The brand could endorse some styles of outdoor clothing, but it clearly subtracted from the value of a range of young executives' suits. Much of this seemed marginal activity for a company whose imagery is about being the original home of denim. The company's profitability subsequently revived with the return to focus of its 501 campaign: wonder at the manly individual who undresses so that his Levi's jeans can be put to heroic uses – stored in the fridge overnight, stripping in the laundrette to wash his jeans, pawned as his last possession of value when his car runs out of gas. The message to anyone within denim's reach is that you are missing out on a legend (and a lifestyle) if you are not part of the Levi's clan.

Objectivity is needed in delimiting the organizational opportunity of a branded legend. A company with the rich experience of Levi's should certainly explore opportunities to foster new fashion concepts with new brands. Clan labels, which offer the consumer the chance to be seen to be voting for particular lifestyles by wearing the brand's badge, are a growing phenomenon as examples like Benetton, Nike, Naf-Naf and Reebok have shown. It would be surprising if Levi's, the company which pioneered the global clothing clan, fails to breed some new labels in the nineties.

Procter & Gamble's Head & Shoulders has proved to be a world class segmenter of a product category. In shampoo marketplaces, the anti-dandruff sector is usually the minority one compared with that of cosmetic brands. However, Head & Shoulders often dominates its segment so convincingly, that it is the market leader. This is a highly efficient branding, but one, as its name implies, whose job is to denote a particular product benefit.

CAA A LOCAL BRAND WHICH IS FIRST CLASS

Citra . . . in the space of a new years, Citra, a Unilever brand, established itself in the eighties as Indonesia's leading cosmetic house. Given Citra's customized rapport with Indonesia's 180 million population, it is one of Unilever's most profitable local brands, putting many of the conglomerate's semi-global brands to shame.

Citra's excellence comes from turning moisturizers and other commodity cosmetics used by Indonesian women into an afford-able branded experience. The inspirational offer is good func-tional products mixed with traditional herbal compounds, such as *mangir*, which are associated with the classical beauty of Indonesian women.

BCB EXAMPLES OF REGIONAL PROBLEM CHILD

Darkie, Le Sancy . . . 'Pandemonium in a toothpaste' is the way that the *Herald Tribune* described Darkie. The brand is a suffi-ciently strong market leader in several Asian countries that Col-gate decided to acquire an interest in the Hong Kong company which owned the brand. Unfortunately, Darkie's trademark, which gives its packaging a prominent identity, is a black man with shining white teeth. While not distasteful to Asians, sec-tions of American society, including some of Colgate's American shareholders find this racist. As Darkie is firmly established in its markets, it could simply have maintained its business for a fair time to come, but Colgate decided to change the name (to Darlie) and the graphics to eliminate racial stereotypes.

As Darkie was born long before national broadcasting organs like the British Broadcasting Corporation were smugly making light entertainment out of Black and White minstrel shows, you could say that Darkie was a sign of its times that parts of our more global community now feel should not be a sign of tomor-row. In contrast, Le Sancy – an economical soap bar from Uni-lever which holds the distinction of being just about the largest piece of soap you can buy – suffered from poor linguistic coor-dination from its conception. After a track record of strong suc-cesses as a new brand in several South American countries, Unilever's search for Asian markets for the brand was somewhat halted by the discovery that Le Sancy sounds phonetically like the offer of 'death to you' in certain local dialects!

A?? EXAMPLES OF WORLD CLASS DECISION TIMES

Timotei, Filofax . . . while Timotei's originality in being the first world class brand to offer nature's mildness has achieved great moments in the eighties, such as the unique distinction for a

Western manufacturer of winning brand leadership in a Japanese market (shampoos), we have already discussed the risk of the brand's image being swamped in our greening age unless Unilever takes steps to incorporate the brand's spirit. Like its elder stablemate Lux, Timotei seems to have bordered on a world class territory of the human imagination, which its corporate orchestrators may not have believed in quite as much as the consumers who identified with it.

Filofax owns the symbol of the organized being. It has the hardware to prove it but resembles early microcomputers in its lack of software. The company has been (critically?) slow to recognize that its future could have been a service club connecting owners with a newsletter around which entrepreneurial franchises such as personalized printing houses could have flourished and an upscale media grown.

Brand valuation exercises – inside transnational corporations

Peter Drucker has identified five trends impacting on the business world which are likely to gain momentum throughout the nineties (*The Economist*, 21 October 1989). These are previewed in Figure 4.2 (and discussed more fully in Chapter Ten).

Within a transnational corporation, overall management of the brand portfolio should now be seen as being concerned with the strategic choice of identifying various flagship businesses, including the selection of a small number of world class directions. It is clear that transnational visions are pushing irreversible trends in corporate focus as far as product unbundling is concerned. In parallel, the essence of brand valuation is to keep control of image unbundling.

In these large corporations – where the annual investment in advertising can run to hundreds of millions of dollars across the brand portfolio – the choice of levels at which product lines are collectively grouped under the same branded identity is now a matter from which the total organizational function flows.

- Reciprocity will become the central principle of international economic integration.
- Businesses will integrate themselves into the world economy through alliances.
- The restructuring of businesses in the 1990s will be more radical than at any time since the modern corporate organisation first evolved in the 1920s.
- Self-perpetuating professional management in the big company will be challenged, as will the definition of effective performance.
- International and transnational political (and economic) issues will tend to upstage domestic ones.

Figure 4.2 Peter Drucker's five trends for the nineties.

The purpose of every major brand in the portfolio should be continually reviewed as the climate of transnational marketing evolves. How worldly is a brand intended to be? Which product categories can its image endorse? What alliances should be entered 'just-in-time'? What 'marketing edges' give the brand its bargaining power? Should the brand be a corporate subsidiary in its own right?

Even the largest business corporations can only afford a few of the long-term and costly investments that world class brands involve. It is doubly important that marketers should distinguish between nurturing prototype world class brands and developing dedicatedly local ones, as the properties involved in brand building (discussed in Chapter Five) differ radically as a function of these objectives. In proceeding with regular budgetary allocations to individual brands on the basis of sales and profits estimates, head office and local offices should also renew the ABC assessments of the futures of their brands. The review process should also account for competitors' brands in terms of both threats and alliancing opportunities.

On Accountability And The Inheritance of Emotions

An introduction to brand building and demolition

Brand building is rather like climbing Mount Everest. It is a matter of establishing first base camp, then second base camp, and so on, eventually establishing five bases in all. Unfortunately, many brands barely get past first base (competitive value) because selling often gains more applause than marketing in Western business circles.

American stockmarkets place quarterly sales hurdles in front of their businesses. European bourses are only a little more lenient. Media experts and investment analysts revel in these opportunities to give business strategies their thumbs up or down by instalment. Obediently, Western marketers have developed many tools for demoting their brands (though most people politely describe it with an opposite word) by bringing immediate sales forward at a net long-term cost to the brand. Tools for demotion include some tactical couponing, most prize and free-gift promotions where these have no connection with the brand's image or function, and almost all occasions where product or service is compromised in a drive to be cheaper.

Selling value, marketing quality (branding's first and second base)

The way to get past the first base (competitive value) is to know where it is to be found, but never to take your eyes off second base (competitive quality). As these are often fuzzily defined terms, it is useful to balance one against the other to feel the distinction.

Consider two brands 'Val' and 'Qual'. Val is perceived by consumers as offering high value and low quality; while Qual is seen as low value and high quality. Both of these brands have an apparent virtue which can also be their undoing.

Val is likely to be at the peak of its sales power. All the commentators will say that it is very impressive, but in fact its future as a business may be near the edge of a precipice. Brands which lose their quality image have been 'milked', sometimes incurably. You may take a brand downmarket very easily and gain temporary sales in the process; but steering that brand upmarket again will be a very costly marketing exercise. Think of how many cars we could sell for Ferrari tomorrow if we cut their price to that of a Ford, and then think of the day after tomorrow.

Qual is likely to have a lot of locked-up business potential if only its value can be improved. As its current business may be seriously underperforming, it is a hidden asset which may fall prey to predators.

High price is only one reason why a brand may be perceived as poor value. Its full benefits may not have been presented appropriately to potential consumers. This situation is commonplace with products where consumers become more discerning as their experience of product usage increases. Or a brand may be hard or costly to find as a result of a lack of distribution outlets. In this regard, most Europeans would understandably say that going to Harrods for a shopping trip is poor value while its only location remains in Knightsbridge. Just as going to Pasadena for a McDonald's was poor value for most people until Ray Kroc franchised it in thousands of locations.

Incidentally, where brands trade heavily on their image, a lower price may reduce the perceived quality of a brand to such an extent that a brand's value also declines! Here is an example cited by George Bull, Chairman of International Distillers and Vintners from the *My Biggest Mistake* column of *The Independent on Sunday*:

> When IDV was first taken over by Grand Metropolitan, I got permission to try to promote J & B within the group. I spent half an afternoon telling hundreds of executives from Watney's, Trumans, Mecca and Peter Dominic what a magnificent whisky it was.
>
> My persuasion worked and J & B promptly appeared in optics all over Britain. But then foreigners, used to the idea of J & B as a luxury premium brand, discovered it was just a commodity Scotch in its native Britain and the discovery was beginning to hurt sales in the rest of the world. So, a few years later I had the embarrassing job of telling my in-house customers that they would have to discourage buyers by upping the price and transforming it into the same premium brand as it was everywhere else in the world.
>
> People outside the drinks business may not appreciate what a serious mistake it was because I'd jeopardised J & B's image, and that's the only asset any drinks brand has – apart from its intrinsic quality – and even a whisky as good as J & B can be hurt if it becomes associated with cheapness.
>
> . . .
>
> The story has a happy ending. J & B is still not a big seller here (in Britain), though an awful lot of people are prepared to pay a premium price for it, but it's the second biggest selling Scotch in the world, and its sales outside the United States have gone up eight times in the last 15 years to more than four million cases. And that's not bad for a Scotch which was virtually unknown until the 1950s, and which depended on the US for 90 per cent of its sales until the 1960s.
>
> (Extract from *The Independent on Sunday*, 25 February 1990)

We can monitor the competitive value of brands by noting what brands people are actually buying. In contrast, the competitive quality of brands corresponds to what people would prefer to buy. While most branders monitor 'value' by subscribing to data on sales trends (like the market share audits of A. C. Nielsen which were institutionalized as far back as the 1920s), sadly few companies monitor quality trends. Yet the techniques to do so have proved their worth for over 20 years. Many of them emanate from work on market models pioneered by Professor Glen Urban at MIT. (Contributions from the Urban school of market modelling range from the book by Urban and Hauser, *The Design and Marketing of New Products*, to the evolution of Express as one of the leading database languages for management decision systems.)

Marketing plans for brands should always be evaluated in terms of achieving an appropriate balance between value and quality. The vast majority of quantitative research today fails to address this balance. Fuelled by modern computers it is oriented towards defining the effectiveness of marketing actions in terms of their short-term sales power.

Until this situation changes, critics of market research will have a fair point when they claim that there is too much research of the past and too little research of the future. Analysis of competitive quality helps to give a future focus which analysis of sales trends cannot do. This search for quality is going to be one of the main marketing trends of the nineties.

At a human level, people aspire to own better things. We neither willingly revert to inferior products, nor do we like to be seen to be failing in our business to keep up with the Joneses. Almost every leading business which has stood the test of time has been committed to the evolution of the quality standard. In department-store retailing, for example, rigorous application of this philosophy proved the making of Marks & Spencer, Britain's leading clothing store.

At a practical academic level, PIMS (the institute for Profit Impact of Market Strategy, Cambridge, Massachusetts) has shown that the most significant factor explaining the long-term profitability of a business unit is 'perceived competitive quality'.

Getting the balance right between value and quality is important for a local brand. It is immeasurably more so for a world class brand on which a transnational company's future revenues depend.

Some people find it mysterious that a world class brand can beat a local brand. After all, as a home player, the local brand should embrace all the benefits of customized targeting. We need to turn to the three remaining foundations of brand building to see why and when world class brands build higher than locals.

Star identity (branding's third base)

Look up to the stars and you participate in an experience which has connected our global community since time began. When world class brands began to develop star identities of their own, they also started to appeal to a universal sharing experience.

The world class ambition should not stop at trying to achieve universal recognition of a name. Symbols, colours, packaging shapes, in fact everything that man's imagination may design can be other flagships for a brand's identity.

Coca-Cola has a fleet of them. It owns (almost) universal recognition of two names (Coca-Cola and Coke, each with a distinctive typescript), the colour red as its corporate livery, two flagship packs (the bottle being 75 years young while the can is 30 years old) as well as various pre-emptive slogans which befit 'the real thing'.

Coke's variety of identifiers are no idle indulgence. They afford an array of communications flagships so that the brand can compete efficiently to stay within mind's reach on different types of occasion. The bottle stands out for more stylish drinking, the can for impact on supermarket shelves. Coca-Cola emphasizes the classical tradition, Coke pronounces modernity.

Identities which trigger a positive association in the minds of a universal public do not come for nothing. They represent a heavy investment which often draws criticism from those who misunderstand the brand-building strategy. Even some of advertising's top gurus have misunderstood identity building, which was bold and new in its time.

Advertising Reality, the book by Rosser Reeves which popularizes the unique selling point, is one of the classic texts of advertising. In it Reeves denounces several examples of commercials as 'the tired art of puffery' whose only message is that of a corporate ego-trip. Unfortunately, he cites one example too many when he selects the back cover of a magazine featuring a Coca-Cola advertisement. There in full glorious colour is Santa Claus taking a soft drink out of the icebox and smiling at the consumer. That is the copy to prompt Reeves into his favourite admonition: 'Where is the proposition to the consumer? Where the Uniqueness? And where the sell?'

With hindsight, Coke's Father Christmas spots, which stretched like an annual Christmas calendar over a decade or more, were a great and successful empathy campaign which associated the market leader with many of the warming emotions of the season of good cheer. Indeed, this campaign did more than that. It built up the colour red as an identity of the brand. This became especially important when bulk grocery sales were transferred from the flagship bottle to the red can. Coca-Cola triumphed in its first half-century partly because of its stylish bottle. Coke triumphed in its next half-century or 'supermarket years' partly because ads (like the one Reeves opposed) painted it red, the designer's colour for maximum impact.

For those who feel that star identities should also be legendary, there is a tale that Father Christmas did not own a standard uniform until the day that Coca-Cola first dressed him in red and white corporate livery on the advertising hoardings.

A second story on misunderstood identities is contributed by Barry Day from a piece in the UK magazine, *Marketing Week*:

> Over the last decade some of the world's most imaginative and elegant advertising has emerged from Japan. This has been inspired by a particular attitude "shitashimi-yasui" which means "feeling close".
>
> A few years ago the jury at Cannes was shown a commercial in which a small dog wandered the streets of a city, while a Japanese voice-over imparted a message unintelligible to us jurors.
>
> We turned to the Japanese juror from Dentsu for elucidation. The ad, he said, was for Suntory Whisky. He explained that the narrator had been saying something to the effect of "Many things live. Be well, everyone. Be well."
>
> Even allowing for what the message lost in translation we were still baffled and intrigued. In the end we voted to give it a prize. This may sound a bit perverse but, in our defence, I think we knew we had witnessed something of quality and originality.
>
> Now knowing a little more about Japanese advertising than I did then, I can see that we couldn't have hoped to comprehend the Suntory commercial. Suntory was selling an attitude, hoping that, if the consumers "bought" the attitude they would, in turn, think kindly of the people who had brought the attitude to them.

In the next few years we will see an increasing number of world class identities adopting 'sympathy symbols' as trademarks because international brand names cannot rely on intrinsic verbal meaning. It is prudent to think of the brand name as an audiovisual symbol. It can serve to connect up customers around the world only if they all find it readily pronounceable. Early world class branders like George Eastman knew this. He christened his camera Kodak because it was 'short, vigorous, incapable of being misspelt . . . and meant nothing'.

Kodak's identity system, nicknamed 'big yellow', remains a source of competitive advantage for the brand today. The ways in which the brand's colours grabbed Japanese attention in the late eighties would surely have made George Eastman proud:

> At a time when Fuji and Konica were committed to heavy spending abroad, Kodak spent three times more than both of them combined on advertising in Japan. It erected mammoth $1 million neon signs as landmarks in many of Japan's big cities. Its sign in Sapporo, Hokkaido, is the highest in the country. It sponsored sumo wrestling, judo, tennis tournaments and even the Japanese team at the 1988 Seoul Olympics, a neat reversal of Fuji's 1984 coup when it won the race to become official supplier to the Los Angeles Olympics.
>
> Kodak's cheekiest ploy was to spend $1 million on an airship emblazoned with its logo. It cruised over Japanese cities for three years, mischievously circling over Fuji's Tokyo headquarters from time to time. To Fuji's chagrin, Japanese newspapers gleefully picked up the story. The Japanese firm was forced to spend twice as much bringing its own airship back from Europe for just two months of face-saving promotion in Tokyo.
>
> Half of all Japanese consumers can now recognise Kodak's goods instantly. Kodak's recent growth puts it within sight of second-place Konica in Japan's market for camera film.
>
> (*The Economist*, 10 November 1990)

As the initial letter of a brand name provides a natural springboard for symbolism, creators of new brand names should choose their initial letter carefully. Maurice and Richard McDonald were fortunate in their surname. They built their restaurant stand round two neon-lit yellow arches which passed through the roof. By making the building a standing advertisement, they pulled in a stream of customers. The 'golden arches' nickname for McDonald's M, conceived 50 years ago, has been working ever since.

Identifying marks should aim to make the most use of the product as its own advertising space. Car drivers spend more time behind the backs of other cars than any other kind of hoarding. Yet BMW is one of the few automobiles to take full advantage of this display area. The company's circular badge spotted at the centre of the rear fascia draws precisely on the eyes' focal point of attention. Such cumulative impact helps the brand to attract so many followers.

Much of the apparatus of branding is an investment in a future rooted in the past. Branded identity is the core of this process. Identifying symbols are the leading sensors in the ways we humanly recall things – memories, experiences, associations and connections for the making.

Think of Esso's tiger. Wherever Esso's image on performance is threatened, the company can rely on a campaign featuring the tiger's power to restore consumers' high performance perceptions of the brand.

Over at Disney, almost every year is an anniversary. Snow White's fiftieth was followed by Mickey's sixtieth. Anniversaries rally the staff as well as the customers. CEO Michael Eisner puts it like this:

> I've probably thought through every year through the turn of the century. Things take so long to do, you have to plant your flag and build your company around it.
>
> An anniversary forces you to reanalyze your life. It forces you to recommit yourself to your vows and forces you to finish all your

Esso's tiger: animal power to the brand.

> projects on time to get them done by the anniversary. . . . Dead-
> lines are probably the strongest creative tool I know of. You've got
> to do it. You have to get your act together. The anniversary philo-
> sophy is much more than marketing.

When a brand's identifying mark is changed beyond recognition, it loses all its power to connect back with consumers'
memories of a brand's history. So symbols which are dynamic
but abstract often prove best for mediating products through
time. Who forgets seeing Colgate's ring of confidence? This
visual image signs off a television message efficiently by attracting your attention back to the brand. Over decades this symbol
has also carried such varied personal confidences as fresh-breath
reassurance and protection for the family against tooth decay.

Abstractly, Nike's 'swoosh' mark (the curly tick which provides a boomeranging pedestal for the brand name) could be a
descendant of Colgate's ring. But its power to the brand works
very differently. If I were asked for the one word which I associate
with the swoosh, I would hesitate between 'energetic' and 'correct'. It manages to convey both, and that is why it succeeds.

Motivational symbols which are at the border of ambiguity
and transparency make identities which consumers like to wear.
They are becoming some of the most valuable properties in the
fashion business.

At its most visible, the identity of the brand can become the
consumer's own advertisement for impressing peers who witness
consumption. Marlboro, as mentioned earlier, was one of the
first brands to owe its existence to such an explicit conception as
'the cigarette for men that women like'.

Unlike local brands, the world class identity also enjoys the
privilege of being able to make cost-effective use of such global
media spots as trackside hoardings at the Olympic Games. Being
seen in the neighbourhood of other world class brands is to
inherit a state of international approval which local brands
cannot muster. Subliminally, historical replays of such global
media events create a cumulative sense of discrimination
between brands with world class status and those with something rather less.

> Alongside the footballing superstars of Italia's 1990 World Cup, the
> serious competitive pitch was reserved for the brand hoardings.

As events turned out, many of these identities looked under-rehearsed to play their part behind the scenes, being handicapped by over-long names or graphic logos designed to exploit media opportunities offering more time or space in front of the audience. In contradistinction, one four-lettered word made effective use of every camera angle. The MARS house colours – dramatic red with gold bordering against a black background – proved to be a stylish flag for the confectioner's global panache. By easily scoring the most global rating points, the Mars branding was the visible winner of the championship.

(On-Hand Communications Ltd, 1990)

When you compare a world class brand which is familiar to a billion people with a new brand known to nobody, identity starts to become a very concrete property. Indeed, if any world class identifying mark does not have a high opportunity cost, it may have spent a wasted journey getting there.

Today, the world class identity has an extra premium wherever it can be associated with products competing in markets which are in a state of transnational convergence. Whether the drive for convergence is stimulated by the concept of a single international marketplace, the race for competitive alliances, or the merging of distribution and media channels, or the mobility of consumers and their aspirations, the world class identity acts as a centre of gravity. This leaves local brands increasingly at risk of looking peripheral to the main marketplace. Companies which already own characters in marketing's global theatre should be careful to explore their best uses. Companies creating new entries should be careful not to circumscribe the business territory of their investment in an artificially restricting way.

Extendible experience (branding's fourth base)

In our crowded communications world, the virgin consumer no longer exists. In an age where the prospective consumer – every one of us – is propositioned by up to 1000 commercial offers every week, new brands have an increasingly remote chance of gaining more than a 5% foothold in a mature marketplace. (See Chapter Seven for a detailed discussion of 'par shares'.)

A human analogy shows why. Few of us can cope with making new friends every day. Once we have settled in to an environment, we tend to reserve an inner circle of friends. We are prone to rely on the familiar because of habit, pressure of time in a busy world, or lack of psychological energy to look for something new. Among our friends, we often compartmentalize the activities which we most associate with them, resulting in a full spectrum of relationships from the broad and open to the narrow and specific.

The challenges that a brand faces in winning our attention are not dissimilar. It may have the twin aims of becoming a familiar friendly experience and creating an impression which will endorse a wide range of activities (products). Branding's fourth base can be christened the 'extendible experience'.

An open contest for the world's most extendible brands would begin with the following question. What brands enjoy strong recognition as top for quality in their image territories, but have failed to realize how broadly consumers may be open to their offerings? Possibly Harrods (because would-be consumers currently have to make an expedition to Knightsbridge), Rolls-Royce (because the range of consumer products is so strictly limited) and Disney (in uniting a market for world class children's products and services) may soon find that their credentials for endorsing businesses are far wider than even their owners have fully realized.

Fostering the spirit of extendibility across a multinational's brand portfolio should now be the top priority along every avenue of business development. There are the branded images which a company already owns, those that might be acquired or shared through a joint alliance, and those that could be created from scratch.

Along all of these avenues, the dimensions of extendibility pose three kinds of question. How extendible will this brand be over time? How extendible will the brand be across countries? How extendible will the brand be across product categories? Designing extendibility into the branding process is likely to be the most sought-after communications expertise of the nineties. Leading multinational branders like Procter & Gamble and Unilever are finding that the concept of extendibility as the hallmark of the transnational brand leads to a total reassessment of the practice of brand building.

A senior Unilever coordinator recently expressed his new marketing mission like this.

> In Europe, our division has a few pan-European brands, a few local brands which will remain that way, but the bulk of our brands which are local today will need to be managed convergently to become true Europeans.

New kinds of questions for would-be transnational advertisers to ask are:

- Is this brand's image transportable internationally?
- If so, how quickly?

These apparently innocent questions can have an explosive impact on the types of communications strategy which are desirable at the heart of a brand's advertising campaign. The 'heritage brand' which relies on building a consistent history of local good is probably the most common type of advertising strategy today. For the purposes of transnational branding, it may now be one of the least cost-effective when practised in its purest form.

Lucozade is predominantly a heritage brand. For decades, this drink built up a special medical image in the UK market. It was 'the drink of convalescence' with the famous slogan 'Lucozade aids recovery'. With masterly timing (just before the arrival of the Aids virus), Lucozade was broadened into a mass-market sports drink which now competes for the total soft drinks market with its unrivalled heritage as a healthy drink. This history makes for an inspired local brand, but it is relatively hard to transport to a new country unless its owners (Beechams), and the distributive trade in each new country, have the patience to cultivate the brand's 'convalescent' image over many years.

Contrast the gestation period for the image of a heritage brand with a classical 'symbol brand' like Marlboro. This image starts to work from the first day of a local launch, thanks to a global ride to fame from the popularity of its universally established symbol (gratis of Hollywood).

For the transnational marketer, owning a non-verbal style communicator *sans frontières* appears a much more attractive proposition than a property which involves the building of a separate heritage trail to link up with consumers in every new country.

It is only in the last few years, as the prospect of transnational marketplaces for almost every kind of business transaction has emerged, that extendibility has become one of the essential bases of brand building. In this new world of marketing, businesses should be prepared for a sea change in their ways of organizing their investment in branding. The company brand which has a reputation for quality has an advantage over another with a fragmented portfolio of brands. The retailer whose branded expertise is the breadth of his merchandise may be better placed than the manufacturer of individual brands. The brand which has its own international communications medium has an upper hand on one that has to rent national TV spots.

Multinationals which are going to survive this period of transformation and emerge as transnational marketers will need several changes of life. One of them, in Bob Heller's words, is 'to become learning companies in which the learning is top-down, bottom-up and lateral'.

The bottom-up aspect of transnational marketing may sound sexy; it should often be the opposite. Local offices of world class companies should be encouraged to have a passion for exchanging details about the competition. Quite sensitive antennae will be needed to detect image attacks which may come from brand extensions by companies which have not previously been competitors. Recently, some multinational companies have seemed to be lacking in the circuitry to connect up even the crudest of sensors on local products.

Operationally, the transnational marketer cannot afford inertia when confronted with a good competitive idea, even if this is launched on the other side of the world. In 1987, Attack, a brand of the Japanese manufacturer Kao, was launched into Japan's domestic laundry detergent market. The good idea was a concentrate that offered four times less powder per wash than ever before. Benefits of the brand included portability and stockability for consumer and retailer alike.

Attack enabled Kao to capture half of Japan's sizeable detergent market in under a year. This was a clear signal that the concentrate detergent phenomenon would roll around the world. It was not heeded by all whom it should have concerned. Fully two years on from Attack's launch, the market research department of a major European office of a leading detergent conglomerate was apologetically complaining that 'we have not seen the launch advertising of Attack yet though we were interested to see it'.

Any transnational marketing company will need to champion lateral communications about competitive threats, or prepare to be cleaned out of its marketplace. I regret to say that I have lost count of the number of stories circulating among expatriates in Japan of the Western marketer who receives his company's latest secret batch of newly improved product, the fruit of several years of R & D, only then to discover that a Japanese competitor had introduced the 'product breakthrough' to Japan's supermarket shelves a few years ago.

Marketing edge (branding's fifth base)

Marketing 'edge' is the fifth base of brand building. Brand builders should plan their marketing edge as the business's long-term rationale for being competitive in the marketplace.

There are three main kinds of marketing edge: economy of scale, blind-product quality and added-value communications. The marketing edges you plan to live with throughout the long lifetime of a brand can have a profound effect on the evolution of the business.

Economies of scale can give brands pricing advantages and trading clout. Brands like Mars, Heinz and IBM have employed this edge to build unique global properties. Those who race to be the biggest should be vigilant about particular types of risk. Any sudden reduction in market demand may hit the economy of the scale leader most. A quantum leap in product

technology can leave the scale leader's manufacturing plant looking monstrously out of date. Experiments with new products
may also be inhibited, as scale criteria can restrict the breathing
space which new opportunities often need to grow.

Visible quality is the kind of edge which shines through however crowded the marketplace and whatever the local language.
It is this edge (in such forms as miniaturization and state-of-the-
art reliability) which has become almost the private property of
many Japanese durables throughout the seventies and eighties.
No brand can compete for long if its company becomes a visible
laggard on quality. This story contributed by Trevor Browne to
Australia's *Marketing* magazine is a typical moral tale:

> In a comparative study of American and Japanese manufacturers
> of air conditioners published in 1983, Professor David Gavin of
> the Harvard Business School reported that the highest quality
> US manufacturer spent three times as much money satisfying
> warranty claims as the average Japanese manufacturer, and the
> lowest quality American producer spent nearly nine times as
> much.
>
> The extra money the Japanese spend on building higher quality
> into their air conditioners came to only half what the Americans
> spent on fixing defective units.

In the 1990s the Japanese also aim to give the concept of a
product range a new meaning. Launches of many new durable
Japanese products are now planned to feature a series of improvements. (As many as eight in the first year of one durable product.)
By this means a company issues its own guarantee of being one
step ahead of, and more interesting than, the competition.

Some executives of packaged-goods companies have been
known to state that their markets are mature ones – technically
speaking, they cannot be improved. When this confidence is
misplaced it can be disastrous. Kao's Attack on Japan's detergent
market has signalled that miniaturization of any bulky product
can set a new standard of convenience preferred by both consumer and trader. We may one day see soft drinks sold as pills
putting any drink effortlessly on-tap in the home. Japanese distillers are already producing whisky taste-alikes (at half the
alcohol level of Scotch to profit from local taxation levels) which

are hard to distinguish from the real thing in tastings where the brand name is hidden.

Wine growers may yet feel the pinch from a Japanese kit permitting the custom design of a drink which meets any graduation point on the wine expert's palate. As biotechnology takes root, it is hard to see how any fast-moving-consumer-goods manufacturer will be safe in discounting the likelihood that there will simply be better made products.

An added-value communications edge adds emotional chemistry to a product, distinguishing it from neighbours which might otherwise be judged as similar in a cold scientific analysis. Added-value images materialize from doubly attentive marketing. First, by developing the most forward-looking and comprehensive sense of the environments (discussed later in this chapter) in which a brand does its business; and second, through realizing sensitive and consistent communications of the brand's image. What seem to be the top six styles of communications adopted by global brands are catalogued in Chapter Six.

A gameboard for world class branding

The marketing function is a practice which involves a mature respect for dealing with uncertainty. The brand builder may simplify the process by concentrating on the establishment of one base (often value). His reward is quite likely to be a transient reverence which does not stand the test of time. Or he may engage in the naggingly unreassuring process of striving to balance five bases which frequently introduce conflicting business tensions, and where the future (not the present) will be the judge of his accomplishment. Corporations intent on being the leading transnationals of the twenty-first century need to let their brand builders know where they really stand.

We have reached the stage where we may profitably integrate the bases of brand building with the criteria for valuation of branded futures (see Chapter Four) and the environments in which world class brands compete. Figure 5.1 depicts a game-

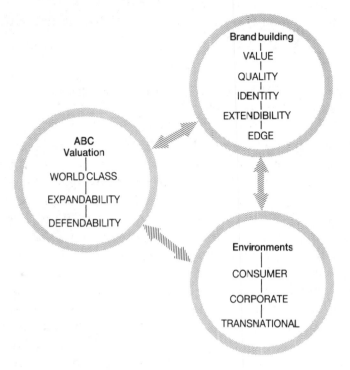

Figure 5.1 The gameboard of branding.

board showing the key strategic pieces for the organization of brands in a transnational marketing company.

This gameboard may help planners in transnational companies to balance the conflicting pressures on resources and identification which evolve with a company's brands and business developments around the world. We can picture the exercise of internal brand valuation as a system for management to decide which brands to promote; by either increasing shares of communications budgets and advertising time or even ultimately reaching the stage of incorporation as an image subsidiary. It can help show which brands to relegate as local businesses that need not concern senior management, provided they meet budgetary and quality controls. It can also show which brands to mix together in ways that are previewed at the end of this chapter.

The valuation of a brand's relative contribution to an organization's future depends on the properties it owns from previous brand building and the environments in which leading identities will need to do business. A brand may need to interact with three main kinds of environment.

THE CONSUMER ENVIRONMENT: PURCHASERS ↔ CONSUMERS ↔ WITNESSES

The consumer environment has a direct impact on every brand which creative communications should tune into. This was discussed in detail in Chapter Three, by posing such questions as: Who is the purchaser? Who (including the purchaser) will be impressed by the choice of purchase? Are impressions stimulated at the act of consumption or by its after effects? Are these impressions indulged in privately or publicly witnessed? . . .

These sorts of question characterize the inner circles of branding which bond a brand to its loyal customers, and its customers to one another. Big brands also interact with outer circles of responsibility which are concerned with such matters as corporate face. These outer issues are usually more transparent when we think of branding's other environments, though most of the keys to branding stem from the images, impressions, communal gossip and lateral associations which a brand seeds and propagates in the consumer environment.

THE CORPORATE ENVIRONMENT: SHAREHOLDERS ↔ EMPLOYEES ↔ CUSTOMERS ↔ TRADE ↔ JOURNALISTS ↔ SOCIETY ↔ GOVERNMENTS

All of these groups hold an audience with the brand and judges it on different criteria. Interactions between these viewpoints – the pros and the cons – are the roots of the 'politics of brands'. No lesser phrase could adequately describe the most expensive communications exercises in history, which find their elected representatives in world class brands.

Shareholders

Shareholders are right to criticize the organization of a corporation's investment in brands on occasions like the following:

- When a company's potential world class brands do not have the recognition they deserve, either because the company has underestimated the expandability of the brands, or because stockmarket audiences do not spontaneously associate the brand with the company.

- When brands are undercapitalized or poorly organized to exploit transnational marketing opportunities in a timely way.

- When a brand is milked (that is, brand demolition of the first kind) or a U-turn is made in a brand's communication image (that is, brand demolition of the second kind).

- When brands (or company employees intimately associated with them) are involved in scandals, particularly where these provoke international or racial tensions.

Employees

The costly communications exercise of a large brand grows up to be increasingly wasteful if it does not give employees a share in its image. Opportunity factors include:

- Pride in continuity of service ideals which are publicly recognized to be world class.

- Commitment to a cause or heritage identified by the brand. When a brand of this kind is promoted as being a company in its own image, the brand provides naturally entrepreneurial directions for developing business alliances around its image.

- The communal sharing of a personal commitment which at its most productive can make the spirit of a large company feel as supportive as a happy family.

- The drive, confidence and enthusiasm of a team spirit which attracts others to you whenever companies combine in trade, mergers or takeovers. And whenever a company's personnel provide a service to the customer.

- The leadership qualities you would expect of a business leader as well as a market leader.

Akio Morita of Sony quotes this inspiration as a founding declaration of the philosophy of his company and brand back in the forties:

> If it were possible to establish conditions where persons could become united with a firm spirit of teamwork and to exercise to their hearts' desire their technological capacity, then such an organisation would bring untold pleasure and untold benefits.

Forty years on, Sony's impact around the world demonstrates that objectives of this quality make a proper aspiration for an organization's communications to rally round.

Customers

At a world class level a brand should not be afraid to have the sincerity to lead the customer. Sony's Morita is also crystal clear on this matter:

> Our plan is to lead the public with new products rather than ask them what they want. The public does not know what is possible, but we do. . . . We refine our thinking on a product and its use and try to create a market for it by educating and communicating with the public.

Morita's logic shows that one way to build a brand's house is to demonstrate the innovative enthusiasm and consistent standard of a leader in the products which you bring to market.

Most of the evidence from advertising history shows that consumers, armed with the large number of votes that repeat-purchased goods afford, take the side of the sincere leader and oppose the me-too imitator.

Trade

In markets served by superstore chains, the retailer is one of the strongest placed to try to seize local branding opportunities. Own labels compete as an offer of high short-term value by being either cheaper or more flexibly tunable to the consumer taste of the moment.

What the trade now expects from manufacturers' brands is a special attraction which is more than a good ordinary product: it expects a brand whose bases have been built carefully so that its image has a pulling power that a trader cannot afford not to stock. As was seen in Chapter Four, one of the biggest opportunities open to the supplier of fast-moving consumer goods is to identify a universal aspiration (such as nature, good health or parenthood) and to team up in alliance with other non-competitive manufacturers to assemble the strongest range of merchandise which fits the brand's megapositioning. Owning the credentials as a number one merchandiser in a selective world class sense is now a summit branding ploy. From different starting positions, the race is on to be the first to fly the flag over these universal ranges. It is a race open to manufacturers and retailers alike.

During the eighties, the franchising of retail units emerged as one of the most effective ways of developing world class brands. The evolution of the franchised unit has two special kinds of strength. First, the working concept can be refined as a practical centre of excellence. Second, growth around the world can be cultivated with just-in-time flexibility to cater for cumulative demand.

Surprisingly, the momentum behind this efficient route to global branding has often come from newcomers, like The Body Shop, leaving established manufacturers and retail chains standing on the sidelines.

Multinational manufacturers should be less wary about experiments with these more concrete ways of developing brands. Paying for the most expensive way of airing a business concept – the television spot – tends to come perilously close to a brander's ritual. The head of one UK advertising agency, Robin Wight, has put it this way:

> In 1965 the budget for a typical brand could be expected to buy 30 minutes of airtime, but now that same budget buys a mere 3.5 to 5 minutes. People's ideas are still frozen in the Sixties. We've got to make ten seconds do the work that 30 seconds used to do. We will have to think about our advertising productivity. We are guzzling media today the way that cars of the Seventies guzzled fuel.
>
> (*Marketing Week*, 24 November 1989)

Journalists

Journalists, governed by the instantaneous pressures of their media, love nothing better than a symbol and a cause. Recently, if you manufactured an alternative to CFCs, you were on a winning roll with the aerosol and global warming. Seldom can there have been such copy for an anti-David-and-Goliath story. The fact that CFC-based aerosols, before they were exterminated by the media, accounted for a small proportion of CFC usage feeding through to an almost negligible increase in Goliath's warmth was not the point of the story. Ironically, 'global warming' and 'greenhouse effects' are not proven phenomena. They are terms coined by scientists who are interested in researching whether the earth's climate is continuing to vary within natural bounds. A decade earlier, many of the self-same scientists were feeding a catastrophe-hungry media with images of global cooling and the advent of a new ice age.

Since causes are often complex, as in the above example, it frequently pays companies to relate to journalists in symbols. The great communicator, Ronald Reagan, demonstrated this best. It is a fact of life that, where reputations are to be made by spontaneous exchanges with the mass media, it pays enthusiastically to avoid being tied down to talk about specific details. On television a correct point passes transiently into the ether whereas a mistake may be replayed a thousand times.

Society and government

Figure 5.2 illustrates the sorts of clubs we, as individuals, belong to in modern society. The privileges of being a member of a club come from an organized body of commitments and causes as well as ownership of material properties and practical products. The

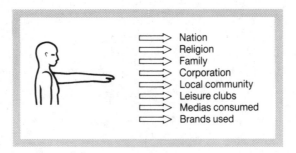

Figure 5.2 Group identities in a world of mass communications.

satisfactions we derive from these human processes often take the form of the insider's contact – the knowledge of a skill or the establishment of an interpersonal role within an inner circle of people. Collectively, these activities also result in presenting the semblance of a united tradition – a visible standing – to outside communities who interact with our own.

We grow so familiar with clubs that it is easy to become almost oblivious to the way they work. To begin to rediscover their purpose – our purposes – it is often necessary to ask the shocking question: what if this did not exist?

What if nations did not exist and we were all world class citizens? We would lose a system, cumbersome though it may be, for identifying priority commitments and styles that represent our national values, and even to some extent our self-images. We would also lose a mechanism, which we might call 'geographical knitting', for working as a united centre of gravity; the combined skills we have to offer, experiences that visitors (such as tourists) feel to be the unique colours of our nation. Europe's 1992 and the decent burial of communism are significant steps towards geographical and philosophical unknitting.

In a very similar way, world class companies worthy of the name will need to prioritize global responsibilities over local ones. The world class brand is a mechanism, which we may call 'global empathy knitting', for sharing universal symbols of warmth. Fortunately for mankind – provided enough people stay media-literate enough to read between the lines – world class brands can be flexibly unravelled, without revolution, whenever they offend consumers. This is a responsibility, a reciprocity of marketing, which everyone involved in the construction of a world class brand needs to feel.

Heady ideals at the core of a brand's transnational image will also involve delicate judgements in such practical matters as corporate PR. For example, acting as a counterpoint to some of the European Community's least practical social commitments is a way of placing a brand on a truly European stage. The Body Shop's petitioning that animal testing should not be a prerequisite to a cosmetic's fitness for human consumption provides an early illustration of the power of the brand lobby to represent alternative branches of European consumerism.

Europes (W/E) ↔ Americas (N/S) ↔ Japan (+neighbours)

The worldwide corporate restructuring of the late eighties has led Professors Bartlett (Harvard) and Ghoshal (Insead) to the conclusion that 'most companies in the 1990s will need to build a different organization to the one they have now'. They suggest that the ideal operating structure for a transnational company will evolve from corporations which meet the following challenges:

- Japanese companies are making formidable progress in moving more assets and resources offshore. Their biggest challenge will be to open up their highly-centralised, culturally-biased management to the growing number of non-Japanese they employ. Remember that the dependency those non-Japanese have on the centre decreases with every increase in local assets, resources and responsibilities.

- European companies have to wrestle with control over widely dispersed and often autonomous national subsidiaries. And they have to coordinate themselves into an integrated worldwide operation. Their twin challenge will be to adapt to 1992 and, at the same time, build a transnational structure for the world market.

- American companies typically have the worldwide network of subsidiary operations that is the envy of the Japanese, and the means of coordination and management control that European companies are still trying to emulate. Their great impediment remains that they are located in the world's largest, richest market, and most still lack the management mentality to see overseas operations as vital assets rather than as appendages to the domestic business.

We may debate whether there is one ideal organizational model for a transnational company. I personally doubt this. For example, small head offices acting as creative think-tanks for franchising centres may compete against HQ offices of the skyscraper style, particularly in service industries.

It is clear however that the vision of an emerging world marketplace will act as a restructuring force throughout the nineties on almost every international company. The effectiveness of a company's total communications budget is coupled to anticipation of its future operating structure. So fundamental rearrangements of communications budgets are becoming vital matters for attention. Brand valuation in the boardroom is a symptom of this, but the cure will involve much deeper thinking than a mere formula for putting the brand on the balance sheet. After all, the prizes to be won or lost on the gameboard of world class branding are territorial identifications in the minds of our global community, expressed by the credentials of transnational businesses – productwise, imagewise and countrywise.

Brands with connections: surnames and forenames

What's in a name? Sony's Walkman, Schweppes' Indian Tonic Water and Ford's Escort illustrate the predominant pattern in branding today – most products are born with more than one name.

An appropriate analogy is to think of brands as having surnames and forenames. Typically, the surname depicts the company or the family which the brand belongs to, while the forename identifies the individual product line. Several ideas flow from this analogy:

- The surname should be the constant guarantee of quality, the credentials which a company (or a subsidiary) rallies round. It should epitomize the breadth and depth of tradition that is founded in the interrelationships between the company's expertise and image, and its audiences' demands and expectations. Forenames represent the different product members of the family. They can exhibit their own personalities, functionally and imagewise, so far as they remain loyal to the reputation and sense of style which the family's name evokes.

- Given a choice between a world class surname or forename, the surname will open more doors. As a family name it can be marketed to unite relationships across borders, whereas forenames are more readily positioned for local nicknames.

Many companies will need to shift allocations of their communications budgets towards family names and away from their individual progeny. Or, as suggested in Chapter Four, where the forename has a world class aura, they should consider incorporating it as its own surname subsidiary.

- Alliances also make more sense at the surname level. Why not Benetton–Disney for marketing a colourful clothes range to children of the world? Transnational business ventures should be blessed by such unions of credentials, products and operating channels. Unlocked equity exists in the lifestyle associated with any world class brand where its product range has been restricted by the logistical capability of a single corporate owner.

Historically, branding's surnames and forenames have often reflected little more than a desire to display who owns whom. As markets converge and world class alliances increasingly make just-in-time business sense, we should expect to see increasingly creative uses of arranged marriages of brands. They may literally aim to offer the consumer the best of both their worlds.

Probably, The World's Six Best Added-value Communicators

Birthrights

Brands now figure among the most valuable property rights in the world. The first to be globally identified with a durable consumer want stands a good chance of being an immortal source of profit. The vineyards of 'champagne' did just that. This marque has become an essential prop wherever important celebrations are staged. Champagne is the master of a global rite. For another product to think of challenging champagne directly would be a heresy among its worldwide public.

It seems that great brands espouse an inner confidence which usually breeds on three peculiar virtues: truth to one's stylistic origins, leadership in the face of a contemporary public and determination never to be outmanoeuvred by a competitor. These seem to be the inner qualities which maintain the heroic identity across generations, but how does it create a permanent place in the public imagination out of a daily commercial routine?

This chapter will aim to stereotype the six most broadly cast ways of adding character values to a brand (illustrated in Figure 6.1). You may enjoy choosing different labels for the emotional causes we survey; anyway, the commonality in their rationales is as interesting as their distinctions. We will also draw parallels with other publicly invested identities where analogies seem to be fitting.

Most world class brands employ combinations of these methods to add to their unique depths of character. Such disciplines of excellence support the branded mission to profit from

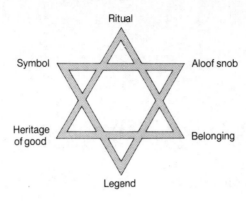

Figure 6.1 The six worldly characters of branding.

being an exercise in continuity of style. In a sense, what begins as a character-building method becomes a mirror to a brand's soul. Great marketers seem to have an instinctive view of branding as a strategy for progressing continuity. They identify strengths for the future in reflections of the past. When a mirror on a brand's public image is broken, a whole dimension of a brand's cumulative investment sinks without trace. Quite simply, as a marketer loses a sense of touch with a brand, his loss becomes mirrored a million times in the subsequent breakdowns of relationships between consumers and their brand.

1 THE RITUAL

Any alchemist who returns to earth today might wisely choose to be a brander. He need look no further for inspiration than that product of ancient miracles – wine. In Champagne and Beaujolais, branders have used the ritual approach to magic crops of gold out of estates that had their beginnings in some of France's least promising vineyards.

Champagne hallmarks its class of occasions from the pick of human rituals, whereas Beaujolais makes a ritual out of its picking occasion. Both of these routes to ritualization have proved undeniable strategies for adding value.

Champagne's image is impregnable because of its recognition as the appropriate symbol wherever people wish to be seen to be taking part in celebrations that are important to their images or themselves. For branders, the Champagne Test is to choose an occasion, and to become so visibly recognized as an essential part of the ritual that people feel that their sense of occasion is diminished without the presence of the brand.

Beaujolais has an enhanced position now that its place in the November calendar is an annual event assured by the international press and the global catering trade. It is a brand which has created its own global birthday party. For branders, the Beaujolais Test is to become the stage managers of a recurring event which catches the public's hearts as well as their diaries. The ideal period between anniversaries should balance frequency against the essential media-warming ingredient that every celebration is seen to be more popular than the previous one.

When rituals dominate a sense of time or place or occasion, they become a brand's social columnist to the consumer's diary. It is the brand's competitive aim to be the first to come to mind at every relevant event in the calendar of consumer life.

A ritual provides a coda on how to behave, within whose rules you may relax. In Japan there is an enormous latent demand for leisure pastimes, but new ones will succeed only if they establish themselves in almost ritual fashions. This is a matter of cultural taste in a society where the Western concept of an individual's public and private lives is not common.

Even the marketing of coffee in Japan did not really take off until it developed its own ceremonies. Today, Japanese coffee houses reflect a variety of social niches which Japanese traditions did not previously cater for, from the French café through the English pub to the German *Weinstube*. In all these settings, the coffee ritual is connected by a tone of informality which contrasts with tea's more formal significance. On Japanese coffee menus you can choose from a large variety of romantic appellations such as Blue Lagoon, the like of which I have never encountered anywhere else and would never be a proper address for a Japanese tea.

Businessmen should take advantage of the disciplinary benefits of rituals. It can be far more motivating for staff to perform a ceremony than to repeat a routine. This is an increasingly important factor for branding to encompass with the growth of service industries. The employee's enthusiasm for a service job

(or lack of it) is often the customer's most telling point of contact
with the product.

2 THE SYMBOL

There are many sources of branded symbol power. Some brands
have adopted images that others, like Hollywood, have already
popularized – from Marlboro's cowboy (for men that women
like) to IBM PC's Chaplin (evoking clumsy ignorance as respectable for executives who might know less about computers than
their secretaries). There are symbols that have been designed to
play on the characters we personify in animals – from the power
of Esso's tiger to the adult humour of Lacoste's alligator (see page
xii). There are products that cut their own distinctive shape in
social circles like Filofax's six-ring symbolism of being highly
organized in the eighties.

The power which symbols bring to the language of branding is
equally diverse. We observed in Chapter Five that symbols as an
expression of a brand's identity are often shared reciprocally with
the consumer. Today the clothier's favourite motto 'you are what
you wear' extends to many other goods; the brands we choose
to consume are often symbolic acts which we want our peers
to witness. In this, we rely on a universal, if subconscious,
understanding of the brand's message to make a statement about
ourselves.

Brands which sum up their qualities symbolically gain
recognition from even the most fleeting opportunities for consumer attention: from poster sites which we drive past, to super-

Abreast of an adult sense of humour.

market shelves which we trolley past. This is only one of the ways in which pictorial languages are different from verbal ones. What may seem crude as a verbal message is often regarded as refined when expressed in visual terms. Look no further than the delicate way in which Lacoste's alligator savages people's breasts the world over. The best symbol is both subliminal and supraliminal.

All the while, the brander should remember that the typical consumer test of a symbol is: how pleasing is it the hundredth time your eyes meet up with it? This helps to explain why the most productive symbols have a certain cleanness of style, a hidden simplicity rather than a showy complexity.

Confucius observed that 'a picture is worth a thousand words'. For the transnational brander the relevance of this saying should now be extended: ' . . . spoken simultaneously in hundreds of different languages'. Historically, the number of brands that were originally conceived as global symbols remains surprisingly few. Even Marlboro's cowboy came as an international bonus from a conception that had been devised for American smokers. As we turn to a new millennium, international symbolisms are likely to figure increasingly as signs of the times.

As branders search more earnestly for globally meaningful symbols, they could usefully employ a triumvirate of commercial designers. It is time to blend the symbolic talents of the American, European and Japanese (Asian) ways.

Americans have created most of the world's leading populist symbols. In doing so, they have drawn on skills that go hand in hand with global domination of the movies and TV programming. Their designs also show a natural talent for the boldest of commercial strokes. Typical of this are the take-away franchises whose buildings need to symbolize their wares against the backdrop of an automobile-transported society with its vast highways and shopping malls.

The European tradition is an excellence in symbols of snob and style. Examples range from the artefacts of *haute couture* marques to the romantic emblems of history. Frequently, home-grown symbols of modernity look remarkably hollow against the roots of history. Pity only the European who finds his lifestyle constrained by such a legacy.

Japanese (and other Asian) designs have proved to be rich in their surprises for the Western commercial eye. Reciprocally, many of the West's designs are increasingly at risk of looking naive to Orientals. The West needs to face up to this before the oriental consumer replaces the American as marketing's centre-fold. The budding global marketer will need to appreciate many sources of beauty, not the least of which is the Kanji alphabet (common to the Chinese as well as the Japanese) as well as the Roman ABC. The discipline of thinking with an alphabet of several thousand pictographs begins with the learning of a sense of artistic order. It becomes a journey through mankind's richest collation of symbolism which over a billion of the earth's people already share.

The opportunities for branded symbolism take on a higher order of influence when we consider the corporate brand. Here is John Diefenbach, CEO of the design consultants Landor Associates, on the coordinated impact that symbol power can give to a company's identity:

> The modern corporation is a very complex structure, and it communicates to its public in many different ways. There is, of course, promotional media – print, electronic, direct mail. But public perceptions are formed by many other, more permanent media: for example, company owned 'visibility assets' – headquarters and branch offices, factories, distribution facilities, retail outlets, signage, trucks and cars, personnel uniform, business forms and stationery, product design, packaging, and point-of-sale displays.
>
> A well-integrated visual communications system uses repetition of design or its elements of colour, line and texture, to reinforce a total impression on the public memory. The logo prominently displayed in an office makes a good strong statement but it is the echoing of its colours or a 'secondary format' on a product or package, or on the business forms, or in employee uniforms, that provides the all important, if subtle, reinforcement.
>
> Airline customers, for example, who are impressed with the graphics on a 747 must not be allowed to forget that airline's identity when they enter the cabin. A good visual communications system will remind them over and over again of the company's unique personality. They may not be conscious of each detail – that the carpeting picks up the secondary corporate colour, or that the china and linen bear the same border trim used on signs at the boarding gate. They may not be aware that the typeface

in the company advertising is repeated on their boarding pass, ticket holder and baggage tag, but each integrated item will contribute to an overall impression of the personality unique to that airline.

A company that successfully employs these visual communications techniques is perceived with more confidence. The system projects a tone of planned cohesiveness, reassuring sense of order. That alone strikes a responsive chord in customers. Without knowing why, they are impressed with the company's togetherness. And this reflects, or course, on their products or services. Products become an extension of the corporate personality; services become less abstract more tangible.

> (Extract from *Branding – A Key Marketing Tool*,
> Edited by J. M. Murphy)

3 THE HERITAGE OF GOOD

Historically, the endowment of a brand with a positive good has been the most successful for branders. By singlemindedly addressing an emotional theme, the feelings associated with a brand can become just as strong as its product functions. Is Coca-Cola valued as a drink, or as the sharing of a friendship? Is McDonald's a fast-food restaurant, or a substitute for a homecoming? Is Disney a children's amusement, or a celebration of family values?

Many brand leaders which have retained their market shares in spite of a succession of competitors with emulative products owe a lot to the heritages which they have built. By being the first to signify such values as health, nature, friendship and safety they have made the most of their products' societal values as well as their functions. The brand that has worked to become a trustee of consumer faith can preclude new brands from being introduced. Emotional attachment is the competitive advantage which a new brand never enjoys.

So how do brands put their emotional signatures on consumers' minds? With symbols like Kellogg's sunshine start to the morning or Johnson's tear-shaped bottle of shampoo which promises baby no more tears. And with slogans like Coke's 'real thing' or Timotei's 'so mild you can wash your hair as often as you like', or even IBM's 'I think therefore IBM'. And by co-opting the help of others like the detergent which comes recommended by all leading washing-machine manufacturers – the indirect message being that the mum who prioritizes safety in gatekeeping for her family's needs should not put herself in conflict with unanimous expert opinion. And, continually, through encouraging the habit of using a brand whose every component has a singleminded devotion to its image.

The success of heritage brands should not blind marketers to their Achilles' heel. On transportation to new marketplaces many heritage brands suffer from a double ignominy. Against established brands they have the disadvantage of the newcomer that only knows how to prove its value over the long term.

Silk Cut is an example. This brand was one of the first to establish itself as a low-tar cigarette in the UK market, where it now enjoys a 20 year history. The brand has been grown into a UK leader by executing a carefully understated style, while patiently waiting for trends in smokers' tastes to progress to its mild side of the marketplace. Its key imagery involves the brand's distinctive mauve-and-white livery together with the brand's puns on mildness. Its name has grown up with an advertising history which began with pictorial metaphors of milder tastes like coffee with whipped cream, and which over the years has developed to such minimalist form as a poster displaying a swathe of mauve silk with a gash in it (no brand name and no copy apart from the government's obligatory health warning).

Silk Cut works in the UK because its heritage is mild virtuosity. The brand's communications reinforce this by being a talking point among media people as well as consumers for daring to progress to the minimalist school of advertising. In other European countries where Silk Cut has only been on offer relatively recently, its advertisers have a challenge on their hands. That they might try nothing more substantial than its minimalist UK campaign makes for some astonishment. In Spain, confusion reached quite a peak as this report from *Euromarketing* shows:

Spain November 1989: *Gallaher revising Silk Cut cigarette ads in Spain* – because many people don't understand the surrealistic approach. Gallaher has been using Saatchi & Saatchi's campaign which portrays swathes of purple silk instead of the brand name.

But Spaniards think the campaign is part of an anti-smoking program funded by the national health ministry. . . .

Today's budding transnational branders need to be careful in
their evaluation of heritage brands. The contrast to make is
between the local heritage, which needs to be seeded from
scratch in every new marketplace, and the heritage of an internationalist which can work to pre-sell attachment to the brand
before its local availability.

The United Colours of Benetton reveals the internationalist at
work. This fashion merchandiser has grown its heritage around
its world of colours which connect up a patchwork of worldly
themes. These include the invitation to make the world a more
colourful place by wearing Benetton's clothes, and the opportunity to join the Benetton clan whose members are visibly
voting for an image of multiracial harmony. The brand's multi-
lingual slogans even start to teach people of the world to communicate with each other.

The greater the ideal, the more important it becomes to share
the sense of commitment with everyone connected with the
brand. The advertising of world class 'goods' takes on a reality
as a total business proposition rather than a mere consumer
message.

4 THE ALOOF SNOB

The aloof snob is the kind of character you meet in more *haute
couture* brands. The occasions when we feel we should be
impressed become the keys we recall when we wish to impress
others. Nobody knows this better than the fashion designer,
whose prestige can be used as the image on all kinds of products
from perfume to luggage to personal stationery.

Aloofness is a vital part of the being of most snob brands.
Nowadays, many Paris fashion collections are essentially loss
leaders designed to sell the maison's perfumes. Similarly, flagship lines claiming to be the most expensive of their kind in the
world make good windowdressing while the brand is busily selling other products. As Karl Lagerfeld, a Chanel designer says: 'If

a dress is too expensive, then there's the same magic in a bottle with the same name'.

I remember reading one particularly furious critique of a recent crop of advertising for the Joys, Obsessions, Opiums and Poisons of this world. The author queried: who were all the goddesses depicted in these ads posing like courtiers to the brands? Surely they were increasingly out of touch with their consumer audiences? They were and are, and that is the point of the genre. Advertising of a *haute couture* marque is not aimed at us, it is aimed above us. Its purpose, like any high art form, is to gratify the upper strata of the human pyramid – including the superstar who may grace the advertisement and the columnists who review her scenery – so that their nods of approval may filter down to us over time as one long spiral of impressions.

The process of launching a new perfume can be likened to the first night of a play. Everyone knows that the views of a handful of critics will be make or break. As Meredith Etherington Smith reported in London's *Daily Telegraph*:

> When Chanel launched Coco, the stablemate of Chanel No. 5, it took over Versailles for the night and invited nearly a thousand glittering and sequinned socialites, journalists and retailers to pretend they were at the court of Louis XIV. An 18th-century ballet was danced in original costumes in the theatre originally built by Madame de Pompadour. The palace was entirely lit by candles; huge urns of roses and lilies cascaded from the walls. The Hall of Mirrors hadn't seen so many people since they signed the Treaty of Versailles after the First World War.

Unlike most styles of branding, the aloof snob can be devalued by too much direct publicity. The most telling case-study for the genre comes from a non-commercial establishment. Here is Andrew Morton's analysis of Britain's Royal Family's progressive exposure to the media:

> For decades the twin imperatives of the Victorian constitutionalist, Walter Bagehot – that the monarchy is to be "reverenced" and surrounded by an opaque "mystique" – were the philosophical justification for a dignified distance between the crown and its subjects. Bagehot's ringing commandment that "we must not let in

daylight upon magic" has served as the text for every (British) monarch this century, including Elizabeth II.

During the 1980s, though, daylight was allowed to flood in as the younger royal generation was seduced by the siren song of television, its risks to the monarchy's position minimised by the sycophants and the illusions of ratings success. Youthful enthusiasm and inexperience triumphed over the cautious example set by the Queen.

In the first decades of her reign the young Elizabeth II allowed television full access to the ceremonial aspects of the royal round – the weddings, Trooping the Colour, the investiture of the Prince of Wales – but kept intact the Bagehotian veil over the private corners.

Daylight was first allowed in when the then press secretary to the Queen, Sir William Heseltine, convinced her that she should allow television to film the royal family at home. The resulting documentary, *Royal Family*, was the hit of 1969, showing royalty with a human face and a sense of humour.

Twenty years on, the architect of that radical departure from the past acknowledged that the original decision may have devalued the currency of monarchy by encouraging the unremitting small change of media interest. In a recent but little noticed lecture, Heseltine, now the Queen's private secretary, asked: "Are they themselves to blame in some degree by admitting the TV camera to their private lives for the making of the *Royal Family* film?"

Certainly, after the wedding of the Prince of Wales and Lady Diana Spencer in 1981 the curtain of mystique was torn asunder, and royalty began to become virtually synonymous with showbusiness. The likes of Michael Parkinson, Selina Scott and Terry Wogan queued to interview the royal family, coyly discussing their private lives while berating the tabloid press for its excesses.

. . .

The popularity of royal television shows – and the wider popularity of the royal family – is not to be doubted, but that is not the point. The decision to appear on the screen for no other reason than to entertain strikes at the heart of the ideological framework that sustains the monarchy and essentially defines the difference between Joan Collins and the Princess of Wales.

The younger generation of royals, with no intervention from wiser heads, saw little amiss with the constant adulatory coverage of their hobbies and their lives. The shallow applause of the ratings was accepted in exchange for the deeper springs of reverence and mystery which are the last defence of the royal family against the pressures of the modern world.

The nadir of this haphazard policy was the *Royal Knockout Tournament* in 1987, which symbolised the drift from constitutional certainties within the monarchy. Prince Edward, fresh from his bruising encounters with the Royal Marines, used a television idea way past its sell-by date, which combined royals with showbiz and sporting stars in a series of rather juvenile games based on a medieval theme. The sight of the Duchess of York, her voice hoarse with yelling, racing around the soggy turf like a sixth-former, or a grinning Duke of York hurling plastic fruit at his wife, did little to burnish the dignity of the crown.

When the former King Farouk of Egypt coined the *bon mot* that by the end of the century there would only be five royal houses – spades, diamonds, hearts, clubs and Windsor – he did not mean that the members of the latter were to be the jokers in the pack. As one member of the royal family admitted after this very public debacle: "If we carry on at this rate we will be like a firework, making a spectacle for a short time and then phut . . . gone."

(*The Sunday Times*: extracts from Andrew Morton's book
Theirs is the Kingdom)

In business it can be very tempting to use the credentials of an aloof-snob brand to endorse other products. Almost always the resulting *nouveau riche* products make some quick sales, but the marketer must constantly question whether newly coined glamour is being stolen from a brand's traditional prestige.

Truly purple-blooded houses in the commercial world, such as the house of Chanel, are constantly on guard to preserve their aloofness. The idea that Chanel could become a popular forename may be the most serious form of imitation which the brand has ever faced.

She has dark brown eyes, black hair and a beautiful smile. A judge may deem her to be fragrant, although she is only nine months old. For the question that is occupying France, and employing several lawyers, is whether she has the right to bear the same name as Chanel, the perfume and fashion empire.

Sandrine Rivat little realised that she was launching a *cause célèbre* when she registered her daughter's Christian name as Chanel last December, or that the Paris-based company would go to court to protect its trademark in a case that could drag on for years.

Until recently, French law dictated that Christian names could be selected only from the holy saints listed in the official calendar, or from the approved gallery of French historical figures.

When Rivat went to her mayor's office, officials not recalling Chanel among this august company, turned for advice from a higher authority. The public attorney took a lenient view, reflecting the modern trend that merely seeks to ensure that the forename is not ridiculous, but asked Rivat to add a conventional name. She added two – Michelle and Arlette – after her mother and mother-in-law.

This diplomatic move did not mitigate the offence in the eyes of Chanel. "Chanel is our property" a spokesman said. "We don't intend to let this commodity be tarnished or banalised. The trademark possesses a commercial value worth millions. The name is the key element in the company's heritage."

The empire devotes nearly 4% of its turnover to chasing off interlopers, mostly small entrepreneurs hoping to cash in on Chanel's worldwide appeal. It reckons to win 95% of the cases, but this is the first one it has had to tackle in which Chanel has been used as a Christian name.

(Stuart Wavell, *The Sunday Times*, 9 September 1990)

5 THE BELONGING

While the advertising of an aloof snob is aimed above us, the 'belonging' employs equal subtlety in asking everyone to join the crowd. In a natural way, the snob and the belonging complement each other. The state 1 (snob move) is aiming above others; state 2 (the belonging move) is aiming for communion with others. We all zigzag between these states, often in the course of a single conversation, let alone as we encounter different audiences as we go from home to office, work to play, child to adult.

Our ways and methods for flipping between these two states include the language we use (verbal communications), the physical gestures we make (non-verbal communications) and the brands we bring on as props (signal of mass communication). Here are some examples illustrating the polarization of brands: Benson & Hedges' Gold versus Marlboro's tribe; Carlsberg's best versus Carling's heros; Burberry's élite versus Benetton's united club; Dior's opera crowd versus Naf-Naf's street conscious; Rolex's *pièce de résistance* versus Swatch's wardrobe.

At the beginning of this century, most of the products with which people adorned themselves had little emotional meaning. At most they had sentimental values which were private and individual. You had to be very rich to make a show and indeed that was often the only message of the rich's products. The century of the moving image, accelerating through films to television, has changed that. Today's brand is powerful precisely when it provides a product with an in-built script. Its power is not merely its prestige or its popularity among its consumers, but the conformity of associations that the brand transports across society. To the consumer of a Rolex or of a Marlboro it matters a lot what the rest of the world sees in these brands. Incidentally, this means that one of the heroic mistakes in marketing is made by those who assume that it only matters what their brand's image is among their target consumers.

Belonging is seldom sold directly. Its bonds with customers must enter either subconsciously or as rebounds from conditioning factors we encounter in daily life. Witness David Robson's parable featuring two of the leading labels in the everyday attire of modern man, blue jeans (the substance of youthful dreams) and the suit (the property of the city gent or as the Japanese say 'corporation man'):

> Blue denim is such stuff as dreams are made of. Heroic material. In a pair of real jeans you feel at one with everything that is young and funky and free and dangerous. And tough. With revolutionaries everywhere. And with the pioneers of the Old Frontier where life was so hard that men had to cut up their tents to make trousers (or was it that they had to cut up their trousers to make tents?). That's what jeans are about. Wear them until they are patched and ragged from hard riding and then continue to wear them when they're quite threadbare. And if you put your money and your keys into the holes where the pockets were and they slide down your legs onto the floor . . . well that's how it is with old jeans.

However, and this is the crux, there comes a time when age or the everyday facts of social life intrude on this ragged idyll and dictate that a wardrobe of tatty jeans, one down-at-elbow jacket and a collection of old shirts – many of which have great sentimental value and a lot of visible interfacing around the collar – is not enough. For you are (or rather I am) thirty-two years old and sometimes I have to attend occasions where it is necessary 'to dress'.

There is something particularly terrible about going clothes shopping when you haven't done it for a long time. You don't know how to choose. You are unhappy because your waist is much larger than last time and you can't quite believe the new prices. After an unhappy day of dithering all over the West End and nothing bought, I ventured into South Molton Street which is where you go when you have decided either that money is no object or that you have no serious intentions. I went into a very charming shop and tried on a pair of corduroy trousers which were quite nice. "These are quite nice", said I. "How much are they?" "Fifty-two pounds", came the reply. I realised that they must be very good – not so much a purchase, more an investment. As I am not an investor I reeled out in the direction of Oxford Street which is probably where I belonged.

For no particular reason I entered the portals of Marks and Spencer and to my surprise, and perhaps on the rebound, found myself drawn to their men's suits all arrayed on their bilingual hangers. I tried on a jacket – lovely. I asked the man about trousers. "What's your inside leg?" he asked. I didn't know. So he did an impressionistic kind of measurement – it's tough to go through the intimacies of inside leg measurement in a shop full of ladies buying cardigans. "Thirty-one inches", he said. I believed him and bought the suit with a sense of relief and a feeling that I'd done the right thing.

I wear my Marks and Spencer suit nearly all the time now. It is smart and much admired and people don't believe where it came from. The jacket is the most comfortable I have ever had. My suit cost me £45. It is grey, 65% wool, 35% polyester. Amply cut and there's a full pleat in the trousers to accommodate middle-aged spread. No garment could be more perfect.

(David Robson, *The Sunday Times*)

Marks & Spencer has belonged for a long time, in Britain at least, at the centre ground for taste in clothes. Never really in fashion or out of it, neither young nor old, just quality to rely on whenever people feel the need to gravitate towards middle-of-the-road convention.

Blue jeans – or more accurately Levi's position between me-too products and designer frills – went through a sticky patch in the early eighties until the brand's advertisers rediscovered its belonging as the cloth of dreams and eternal youth. The recent series of Levi's 501 campaigns was born out of consumer research which asked people to describe their fantasies and the ways that clothes might be part of these scenes. The young man who strips in a launderette to his boxer shorts to wash his Levi's . . . the cowboy who asks the inn's hostess to preserve his Levi's in the fridge overnight . . . the lad who pawns his Levi's to buy some petrol so that he and his girl can drive on home . . . the has-been (and couple) rescued by a passer-by who uses his Levi's as a tow rope until the old car's rusty towbar (not the Levi's) breaks leaving the girl with a new man. Such scenes with the product as hero go to work on the popular imagination both collectively and individually. The cultural message for anyone who feels young at heart is that you may be missing out if you're not a member of the brand's club.

6 THE LEGEND

Legends inspire a feeling of pride. What can be more public proof of your own discernment than sharing in a legend? Whether you are employed to work on a legend or you own part of one as a consumer. Today, any legend of universal repute may have some latent potential as a commercial property.

In what we may call the Aladdin's cave of marketing, the business genie hunts for old identifying marks – names and symbols of global renown – which will bring all the right credentials to products in the corporate portfolio. Being the 'original one' can turn a product of conspicuous consumption into one of the world's most valuable property rights. Since the day in 1988 when Nestlé paid two billion pounds for confectionery brands acquired from Rowntree, the value of the brand has been stamped indelibly on boardroom agendas of consumer-goods companies everywhere. A legend which has been kept bottled up from a potential global marketplace may be priceless. Consider what the claim to be the original Pilsner could be worth to the world class brewer:

> Pilsner Urquell is the pale bitter Czechoslovakian brew that has long been counted among the world's finest beers. Along with the well-known Budweiser, a heavier dark beer that hails from southern Bohemia, Pilsner Urquell ranks as one of the rare Eastern European products with a well-known brand name and a high-quality reputation to rival its best Western competitors.
>
> Almost from the moment brew masters in Pilsen invented the clear, slightly bitter style of lager in the mid-19th century, Pilsner Urquell has been one of the region's key exports. The town had been home to dozens of tiny brewing houses since the late 13th century, but when the city fathers pooled their efforts to form one large municipal brewery in 1842, the new style of beer was born.
>
> By applying what was then a radical new technology to the traditional ingredients of hops and malt, Pilsen's brew masters created a golden, transparent beer in an age when other brews were dark and murky. While imitation 'pilsner style' beers sprang up so quickly that the word soon became generic for all clear lager beers, Pilsner Urquell (the name means 'Original Pilsner' in German) soon found markets in Vienna, Paris, London and the United States.
>
> After decades of indifference – Communist authorities all but ignored the historic brewery, preferring to pump money into steel plants and other favoured heavy industries instead – the return to a competitive economy has sent Pilsner Urquell suddenly soaring back into the limelight. No sooner than the December (1989) revolution ended than the company began taking steps to set up its own marketing arm.
>
> For the first time in nearly 40 years, the company will play a major role in overseeing its own marketing and sales effort overseas. "We will have to put tremendous efforts into advertising, which no company has ever done before" says a spokesman for the brewery. But even that only scratches at the surface. So many Western joint venture enquiries are flooding into the company's cramped offices in Pilsen that the entire structure of how the company sells to the West will have to be reformed.
>
> (*International Management*, August 1990)

The building blocks of legends are symbols of tradition, so it should not be surprising that branding often trades in the most established marks of man.

> The creative use of anthropology is being explored by Judie Lannon, research director at JWT Europe. "We share myths, whether they are Nordic, Latin or Anglo-Saxon. It is one of the most fascinating areas for developing pan-European advertising."
> The blonde Nordic image created for Timotei shampoo is a case in point and illustrates the transnational power of myth. It even works in Latin countries where most people have dark hair. "It is part of the Prince Charming myth and partly industrial society's nostalgia for Arcadia," says Lannon.
>
> (*Campaign*, 24 October 1990)

Probably the easiest way to create a legend is to make distant your commercial alibi. Social brands need a perceived country of origin so that you know the ancestry you are sharing. Foreign images also tend to make greater talking points than local ones. Look at some of the images we drink up. Foster's as the spirit of the Australian male has hyped its way across the world to become one of Australia's most public ambassadors. Bacardi rum trades on the image of Caribbean sun-lovers. Perrier's French style put the sex into mineral water during the eighties. These lubricants have made the most of their national stereotypes to become international superstars.

Aqua Libra takes the creative process a step further. Its Swiss pedigree of healthy stock is as much the brand's invention as the product's cocktail of juices, as Ian Fraser of London's *The Independent on Sunday* tells:

> Callitheke, the company set up by Grand Metropolitan specifically to market Aqua Libra and develop other premium-priced health drinks, believes the brand could become the Perrier of the Nineties. Perrier had many advantages when it arrived in this country (Britain). It had existed in France for a number of years and could build on its Frenchness. Aqua Libra had no such heritage, so Callitheke decided to invent one.
> To create the impression that the drink already existed in Switzerland, which is renowned for its healthy population, Callitheke set

up a fictitious company in Geneva to licence the drink in Britain. This deliberately misleading ploy worked for four years, but must now be dropped as ginseng, one of Aqua Libra's key ingredients, has recently been prohibited under Swiss law.

When the product first appeared in 1986, Callitheke did its utmost to ensure it entered consumer folklore by the back door. A lavish launch which would have alerted the public to Aqua Libra was avoided. Instead, it was quietly slipped into health food stores and Harrods health bar, then to selected restaurants, and was only distributed to supermarkets and advertised after two years on the market. That way neophytes would think they had "discovered" what they thought was already well-known to a select band of connoisseurs.

For an example of a company which has had longer to consolidate its legendary origins, consider Fraser's description of Crabtree & Evelyn:

> While Crabtree & Evelyn established its first marketplace in America in 1970 and only opened its first shop in London in 1980, all its products look quintessentially English. Sales literature is interweaved with quotations from diarist John Evelyn (1620–1706), who has nothing in common with the company apart from an interest in herbs. The packaging is flowery and scented, and the shops resemble ancient apothecaries.
>
> While the company is perfectly open about its origins, it still manages to perpetuate a rather vague assumption among its customers that it is English. It has eight shops in Britain, more than 2000 in America and is present in 22 countries, a success that can be largely attributed to the gift-buying public's love of sentimental English imagery.

In his *Handbook of Advertising Techniques* Tony Harrison adds these clues on the importance of mythology when positioning products of conspicuous consumption:

> It is in fact very typical of successful conspicuous consumption products that they have their own mythology – like the Dunhill white

spot, like the RR nameplate of Rolls Royce that used to be red but became irrevocably black on the death of Henry Royce in 1933. Successful advertising for such products builds the mythic quality. It is, for instance, not unusual to find lengthy product copy in ads for wines, whisky, brandy and so on. Read it carefully and you will realise it is not giving you hard product facts on which to base a logical judgement, it is skilfully weaving a cloak of romance and legend around the product. And at the same time it is giving you titbits of information to fascinate or bore your friends with.

If gurus of the corporate image are correct, legends play an even deeper role in establishing organizational traditions. It is tempting to explain the use of legends in thoroughly organized companies as the glue which makes corporate and consumer culture inseparable. Advisedly, Wally Olins chose to begin his book *Corporate Identity* with a chapter called 'The Invention of Tradition', a term borrowed from a historian's tome edited by Hobsbawm and Ranger. Here is Olins on the subject:

> In a brilliant series of essays Hobsbawm and Ranger, and their contributors show how throughout history rituals, symbols, visual imagery of different kinds have been invented by nations, sometimes unofficially but quite often as a matter of policy, in order to create new loyalties, obliterate old ones, mark out territories, reinforce ideas and initiate new ways of doing things. . . .
>
> No nation and no century has been immune from inventing traditions. France, amongst European nations, has perhaps been the most prolific. It has, after all, had five republics, two empires and about four kingdoms, depending on how you count them. Some of these changes of regime have been initiated with the clearest symbolism.
>
> The creation of the first French Republic was celebrated not just with a change of flag, from fleur-de-lys to tricolour, but also by the introduction of a new anthem – the Marseillaise – a new system of weights and measurements – the metric system – and a new calendar – with new names for the months.
>
> The modern multinational is quite as complex as the nation state, in some ways more so. The issues involved in motivating people are much the same.
>
> How do you get people to understand what an organisation is about, to accept its behaviour pattern, to accept new ownership, new management styles, new names?

Although the language used to describe corporate activity is very different from that normally used by historians, all these issues are the same.

A corporation will only work properly if the people inside it have a sense of belonging, if they are proud of the organisation and what is does, if they share some kind of common culture, if there is an agreement about what is and what is not acceptable behaviour within the organisation, if they understand explicitly and implicitly the aims and ambitions of the whole business.

This will not happen in a large organisation if things are left to chance. In order to create loyalties, the organisation has to manu-facture the symbols of loyalty: the flags, the rituals, the names. The organisation must celebrate what is is and what it stands for through rituals and ceremonies. Affirmation of faith must be followed by constant re-affirmation.

Museums, company history, buildings in the corporate style, work-clothes, major events based around anniversaries, or pro-duct launches have to be a significant part of the rhythm of cor-porate life. Everything that the company does, everything that it makes or sells, everything that it builds, everywhere it operates, everything that it writes or displays, should build up the corporate spirit, the corporate identity.

Every quest for identity is about tradition in the making. There is fact and fiction in every great communal inspiration of man because that is the way legends humanly circulate. It is the human capacity to communicate in dual mode – the emotional alliteration entwined with the functional descriptive – which separates man's identification with ideas from that of today's computer and tomorrow's robot. Symbols of emotion are bridges to the collective imagination; group morale flows from a shared belief in identity.

If we view a brand's hallmark as a kind of mental cooperative where consumers' imaginations belong – and capitalism rents advertising this licence in return for financing the bulk of mass communications this century, from the printed word of news-papers to the visual image of television – then we should not criticize businesses which fantasize traditions as part of their clarion calls. Indeed we could say it is the prerogative of com-petitive businesses to create legends, against which such societal balances as free markets, consumerism and the law should delineate the fantasist from the forger. By and large, the open-ness of mass communications is proving to afford consumers a fair deal of protection. It certainly seems a better way than the twentieth century's other great system for structuring the spirit of human enterprise – communism.

As a Scot I cannot leave the invention of tradition before citing Hugh Trevor-Roper's essay on the English invention of the kilt and the Scottish invention of tartans. The period to review is 1754–1820. In the kind of information-poor society existing at that time, a manufacturer could forge a tradition which became a national heritage largely through collusion with a single pressure-group posing in the guise of a learned society:

> It was in the years 1757–60 that the elder Pitt systematically sought to divert the martial spirit of the (Scottish) Highlanders from Jacobite adventure to imperial war. . . . These Highland regiments would soon cover themselves with glory in India and America. They also established a new sartorial tradition. For by the "Disarm-ing Act" of 1747 they were explicitly exempted from the ban on Highland dress, and so, in the thirty-five years during which the Celtic Peasantry took permanently to the Saxon trousers, and the Celtic Homer was portrayed in the bardic robe, it was the Highland regiments alone which kept the tartan industry alive and gave per-manence to the most recent innovation of all, the Lancashire kilt. . . .
>
> The idea of differentiated clan tartans seems to have originated with the resourceful manufacturers who, for thirty-five years, had had no clients except the Highland regiments but who now, since the repeal (of the Disarming Act) in 1782, saw the prospect of a larger market. The greatest of these firms was that of William Wilson and Son of Bannockburn. Messrs Wilson and Son saw the advantage of building up a repertoire of differentiated clan tartans and thus stimulating tribal competition, and for this purpose entered into alliance with the Highland Society of London, which threw, over their commercial project, a cloak, or plaid, of histori-cal respectability. In 1819, when the royal visit (of George IV to Edinburgh in 1822) was first suggested, the firm prepared a "Key Pattern Book" and sent samples of the various tartans up to London, where the Society duly "certified" them as belonging to this or that clan. However, when the visit was confirmed, the time for such pedantic consistency had passed. The spate of orders was such that "every piece of tartan was sold as it came off the loom".

So Cluny Macpherson, heir to the discoverer of the Ossian, was given a tartan from the peg. For him it was now labelled "Macpherson", but previously, having been sold in bulk to a Mr Kidd to clothe his West Indian slaves, it had been labelled "Kidd", and before that it had been simply "No. 155".

Just-in-time Market Research

Introduction

When John Micklethwait nominated 1988 as 'The Year of the Brand' in *The Economist* he had this to say about market research:

> Market researchers claim that they too can help the would-be brand builder. The trouble is that too few brand managers use research in the same way scientists do – to test their hunches rather than to help form them.

Throughout the eighties, I felt the same as that while I was helping to organize market-modelling systems and data collection on brands in over 40 countries. Business principles that I can recommend from the experience of participating in a team which has structured information from over a million hours of consumer interviews on brands are:

- Brands can only grow from continuity of strategy at the heart of the organization. The market research process should be the testing of next steps. Envy the Japanese company which is organized to keep a close feel of the marketplace. Pity the Western company with departmentalized executive functions where facts are expected to be conveyed in black and white. As so often, Sony's Morita says it best: 'Marketing is really a form of communication'. The first motivations for market research should be to test hunches. The second should be to explore future scenarios concerning a brand's environment relative to its competitors.

- Always test your new business concept in the smallest possible way that will give it a fair airing. When you are developing a global business, a blockbuster local census will give you an exhaustive small picture of something you do not really need to know. What you need are 'dipstick' reactions from consumers around the world.

- Use research modules that offer systematic connections with past and future research. Tests should continually simulate whole concepts, as far as they have been developed. Consumers do not respond to a brand mix in the same way that they respond to the sum of its parts. If they did, branding would not be the powerful force that it is.

This chapter will aim to live up to this philosophy by illustrating the purpose of some of the dipstick research modules which I found worked. This is not intended to be a comprehensive catalogue. My aim is to convey a spirit of just-in-time market research which can help world class branders keep one step ahead of the competition.

Most of the underlying technology which I will review, together with results quoted from a 'global databank' in the next section, emanate from systems developed in the eighties at Novaction, a Paris-based consultancy specializing in international marketing models.

The techniques discussed are ordered according to the approximate sample size required per market, beginning with the smallest possible sample size $(n = 0)$.

Detecting (n = 0 per market)

The idea of a par share model is to forecast the share that the next entrant in a mature market is likely to achieve on the basis of past experience. It helps to prioritize market opportunities and risks across a portfolio matrix of target countries and product categories. At first, it usually brings bad news.

Today's par share destiny of many new brands is 5% or less. Branded excellence or exceptional marketing activities are

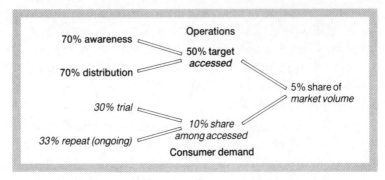

Figure 7.1 Par shares for a new brand.

becoming necessary to beat the pars shown in Figure 7.1. Every marketer needs to get a feel of these numbers and the aspects of the market entry process which they measure. A marketer of a new brand is immediately confronted by four goals. Complete failure at any goal will terminate any prospect of ongoing business. First, consumers need to be made aware of a brand. Second, they must be able to find it in the shops. Third, they should be induced to make an opening 'trial' purchase. Fourth, except in one-off markets, you have to battle to retain your new consumers' loyalty towards the brand throughout all future buying occasions. Let us name these four: awareness, distribution, trial and retention.

As the launch of a new brand proceeds, its performance is likely to fluctuate for a period; typically between one and two years if the product category is bought at least monthly. Only after that will a relatively stable picture emerge. Figure 7.2 illustrates one of the common build-up patterns that can result.

In the battle for awareness, our new brand begins as an unknown identity, typically progresses to a peak level of awareness during the launch and then falls back a bit as some people forget about the brand. Distribution may follow a roughly similar shape, with its peak tailing off slightly as some retailers decide that the brand is not selling fast enough to their customers. Trial is a cumulative measure as it is best defined to be the percentage of target consumers who 'ever' try the brand. Retention decreases before steadying, as many trialists return their loyalty to their regular brands. The market share potential of a new brand, which researchers aim to forecast, is the level at

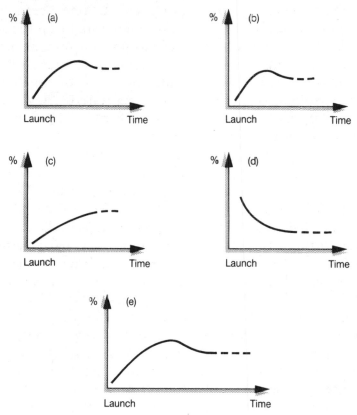

Figure 7.2 The performance of new brands takes time to stabilize: (a) awareness; (b) distribution; (c) trial; (d) retention; (e) share.

which the new brand's business will become relatively stable.

While our marketer's four goals are not totally independent, we may consider them in pairs. Awareness and distribution largely reflect the spend and clout which a manufacturer can afford in launching the brand by means of such marketing operations as advertising and sales-force activity. Trial and retention reflect the intrinsic consumer demand for the brand's competitive offer, from image promised to product delivered.

Data from thousands of brand launches over the past two decades, assembled as an 'experience databank', shows that manufacturers are doing rather well if they achieve pars of 70% consumer awareness and 70% distribution. Multiplying these figures together, we can estimate that only about one half of target consumers are likely to gain access to a new brand in the sense of knowing about it and being able to find it in the shops.

Our databank reveals even lower pars for consumer demand. In terms of the long-term build-up of the percentage of target customers who make at least one purchase of the brand, a marketer is doing well to achieve a trial rate of 30%. Among triers, retention of 33% is the par for future loyalty (which can be placed in context by the fact that most consumers in mature markets tend to have a personal repertoire of three or more of the market's brands). From the product of these pars for consumer demand, we see that a new brand typically gains 10% of the business associated with consumers who have access to it.

Accessing half of consumers and gaining 10% of their business means that the bottom line from the process of market entry for a new brand, amalgamating the effects of marketing operations and consumer demand, is the 5% par share – in other words a somewhat underwhelming one-twentieth of the marketplace.

Naturally pars vary. We ploughed through our databank to discover patterns in trials and retentions for new brands, reflecting variations in consumer demand. Two particularly significant phenomena emerged. First, there are measurements classifying the competitive structure of a marketplace which condition the likely consumer demand that any new brand will achieve. Second, there are specific measures of a brand's performance which combine to rank as the 'top predictors' of how its competitive offer will be perceived by consumers – descending from excellence through par to mediocrity.

HOW CROWDED IS THE MARKET?

Any student of the databank soon gets a surprise. The intrinsic consumer demand for a new entrant in an established marketplace turns out to be largely independent of product category or country. These factors existed in our databank, but proved to be of no significant help in predicting par share. The classifications which do influence a new brand's entry potential are all concerned with market crowdedness. Figure 7.3 shows the four principal ones.

Intuitively, there are two sorts of market crowdedness to

- Share of the brand leader
- Share of the second brand leader
- Number of brands needed to capture 80% of the market (sum up the shares of the largest brands, how many are needed to account for 80% of the market?)
- Number of brands in typical consumer's repertoire of purchasing choices

Figure 7.3 Measurements of market crowdedness which condition the potential of a new brand.

beware of. If the brand leaders themselves only enjoy small market shares, then the offers available to the consumer are already so fragmented that a new brand is unlikely to find a way of uniting a broad franchise. If individual consumers already have experience of a large number of brands which are competing for the next purchasing choice, then the loyalty that any single brand can expect to command diminishes.

At present (early 1990s) we can record how crowded the typical consumer-goods market targeted by multinational companies has become. Today's typical market, resulting in 5% par share for the next entry, measures up like this:

- 20% Brand leader
- 12% Second brand leader
- 10 Brands capture 80% of market (summing up the shares of the largest brands, 10 were needed to account for 80% of the market)
- 3.25 Brands in typical consumer's repertoire of active purchasing choices.

Some international companies dismiss the costly idea of developing a new brand if they know from the outset that beating 5% would require an excellent performance. They prefer to look for markets where the share potential for new brands is twice as good. If a market has the following structural profile, the par share for a new entrant is 10% (that is, the market's gap for a new brand is twice as large):

- 33% Brand leader

- 20%   Second brand leader
- 4   Brands capture 80% of market
- 2.25   Brands in typical consumer's repertoire

BENCHMARKING A NEW BRAND'S FUTURE PERFORMANCE AGAINST PAR

An exhaustive search of our databank revealed a group of five measurements (shown in Figure 7.4) which are collectively the best identifiers of a new brand's ability to beat par through excellence or to underperform due to mediocrity.

Par share modelling has two particular modes of use. First, a marketer can make alternative scenarios on the benchmarks which a new brand might achieve. The models help him to screen markets for opportunities and to understand his margins for manoeuvre. For example, will financial objectives only be met if the new brand is strong on every benchmark, or can a business be grown from a brand which can afford to race into a market from a starting position as an average competitor? Second, as a concept for a new brand takes shape, the model can track its execution by replacing scenarios with actual measurements of the benchmarks. These can be obtained from consumer interviews using standard market-research procedures.

MARKETING REWARDS

How far do developments of new brands vary around par? Out of any five new brands with similar marketing aims (that is, commanding similar price premiums, obtaining similar levels of

Figure 7.4 Measurements for testing sales power of a new brand.

awareness and distribution and entering equally crowded markets] our databank suggests that the best marketing execution is likely to gain twice as much share as the worst one. Put another way: among any five marketers aiming at 5% par share markets, the winner is likely to achieve 7% share by developing a brand mix with a strong image and strong competitive quality afteruse, while the loser is likely to retreat from test market with only 3.5% share.

The rewards for skilful choice of target marketplace are also of a similar magnitude. For example, after smoothing out different market values, our databank shows that a marketer who is logistically free to choose which country to enter first of Germany, France, UK, Italy and Spain will be rewarded if he chooses the least crowded market with a share which is twice that he would get if the most crowded market is chosen.

WHEN DO PAR SHARE MODELS FAIL TO WORK?

Market norms are only norms. Exceptional new brands, playing outside the precedents of a marketplace, can obtain breakthrough results. They occur infrequently. In our global databank less than 4% of launches were breakthroughs.

Fortunately, the most common type of breakthrough brand is easy to spot. It offers a quantum leap in product quality which is so clearly visible to the consumer that it is easy to advertise. Richard Foster of McKinseys calls this 'the attacker's advantage of being on a new technological S-curve'. Japanese electronics manufacturers used this technological force to advance across world markets over the past two decades. It was noted in Chapter Five that other Japanese companies like Kao are starting to exploit biotechnology's promise of miniaturization to attack such everyday products as laundry detergents.

For the marketer, a risky kind of new brand is one which involves a product breakthrough which consumers can only evaluate when they use it. The crowded-market syndrome means that brands of this kind increasingly risk being the victims of a trial-purchasing trap. The new brand needs a strong emotional appeal of its own to gain a first purchase at the expense of consumers' favourite brands. But, the variety of images catered for in a crowded market reduces the new brand's opportunity to communicate to broadly based emotions.

One way of circumventing the trial-purchasing barrier is to reverse the normal allocation of launch expenditure so that most of the introductory budget is spent on sampling instead of advertising. Marketers who do this are staking their business on the commitment to the consumer of the excellence of their product. The risk is that the new brand will be too fragile if competitors quickly catch up with the product technology.

The importance of new brands should not be exaggerated anyway. Most of the evidence from par share databanks, especially that relating to the concept of the crowded marketplace, points in the same direction. Marketers should now explore every opportunity to extend established brands before creating new ones.

Directing the balance of competitive quality and value (n = 50+)

Every branded investment depends on a fundamental management policy – what is the continuing strategic intent of the brand in terms of its balance between competitive quality and value? The way this question is answered has a direct effect on evolution of products developed under the brand's banner, as well as the kinds of marketing activities which will be most effective in supporting the brand against its competitors.

Marks & Spencer began life as a penny store – every product you saw was on sale for a penny. This was the way that the business originally gained its foothold. It was the election of a new strategy which was to transform the retailer into Britain's best-loved chain store.

As far back as 1920, Marks & Spencer developed a philosophy which the Japanese were to reinvent several decades later. The aim was to develop continuous relationships with suppliers who would then be asked to improve their offer at regular intervals. The distinguishing feature of this policy was that Marks &

Spencer would choose, at each of these steps along the learning curve, whether the next improvement should be in terms of better quality or better economy. Through control of this strategy, Marks & Spencer determined that it would always stay quality steps ahead of competitive retailers in its marketplace.

Japanese marketers have convinced me that the most practical product ideal is to be many quality steps ahead of the competition in your planning, and one quality step ahead in your current market offer. The idea is to refrain from offering unnecessary product excellence which consumers may not want to pay for, while keeping a marketing edge up your sleeve so that your competitors remain destined to be followers.

We have seen that product quality is only one major component of the competitive theatre which influences consumers' decisions, since brand images interact with naked products. Fortunately for marketers, an overview of competitive quality and value in a specific marketplace can be mapped out from moderate sample sizes ($n = 50$) of consumer interviews. As a brand is extended across different product categories and countries, it is important to separate out different views of a brand by its various consumers to see how the view of each is changing. Otherwise, a brand's image can easily slip over time to its lowest common denominator.

My recommended way of portraying consumers' views of the quality and value of competitors' offers in a marketplace may look complex. It is worth investing in mentally, because it facilitates comparisons of different marketplaces. It reveals patterns, which the marketer needs to interpret as specific strategic signals.

Figure 7.5 shows the coordinates of brands, denoted by *. Consumers' average perceptions of a brand's competitive quality are represented by the vertical axis, while relative price is plotted on the horizontal axis. Computations have determined a value contour which has been drawn to connect points of average value in the marketplace, so that high value is represented by perpendiculars above the contour.

Normally, the market's bestselling brand is regarded by polled consumers as offering the highest value. If any poll shows it isn't, its lead is usually in decline. Figure 7.5 portrays *1 as a particularly strong market leader. Consumers perceive it as offering

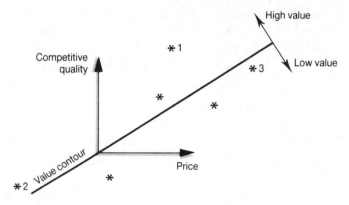

Figure 7.5 Balancing quality and value in a brand's
competitive offer.

the best quality as well as the best value. Arguably, it has two
main sources of rivalry. *2 is a cheap brand which offers strong
value in spite of below-average quality. We may anticipate that
this brand will try to gain ground by making consumers more
price sensitive (rotating the value contour anticlockwise). It will
enjoy non-image-building activities (for example, cheapening
product, price cuts, games promotions). *3 is also a potential risk
to the leader. Although *3 is not very competitive in today's
market, it may have the means to grow its image (by improved
product or sympathetic advertising). It might realize a premium-
quality position, with its high price being part of its exclusive
image.

Figure 7.6 shows two more market patterns which are fairly
common. In Figure 7.6(a), the bestseller *1 has a relatively weak
grip of its market, as the premium brand *2 is offering better
quality. In general, the highest quality brand has the best credentials for extending into other markets, as well as the opportunity
of increasing consumers' quality sensitivity (fuelling aspirations
towards the brand). Figure 7.6(b) shows a market which is
dominated by a cheaper brand and where the quality standard is
comparatively underdeveloped.

Research of this sort can help to chart a brand's competitive
progress as well as stimulating guidelines for action. For example, a brand which occupies a premium position should never

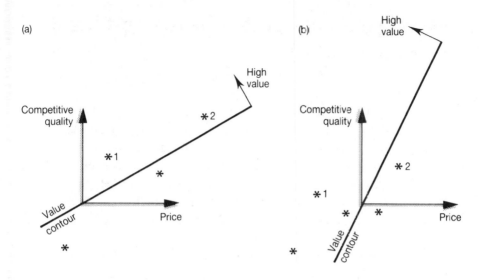

Figure 7.6 Market battles: (a) quality; (b) price.

lead a price war. This is likely to tip the value contour against it. Indeed, if it is known that other brands are likely to indulge in a price war, the premium brand should consider whether it can justifiably take an opposite stand. It might employ an advertising campaign which states that 'price could be cut but not without reducing the quality of the product's ingredients, which is *not* an action this brand would even consider'.

For the marketer who is tempted to extend a premium brand to another product category, it is worthwhile checking that consumers' value-priorities in the new category have a certain correspondence. Extending a premium brand into a category where the whole balance of the marketplace is orientated towards price sensitivity is a risky strategy as the cheapness of the new category may rub off on the parent brand.

Internationally, as brands are increasingly coordinated across countries, it is clear that a common marketing strategy can only begin to work effectively if the brand's balance of quality and value against competitors in each national market is largely similar. (The example of J & B in Chapter Five illustrated this point.)

Identifying with global hearts and local faces (n = 200+)

The successful cultivation of international brands – whether conceived to represent companies or individual products, franchises or product ranges – depends on attracting a lot of marketing enthusiasm for the ideals which are to be at the heart of the brand's image. A winning global brand must be both true to its heart and caringly sensitive of its presentation of local faces which encourage communities to perceive it as a warming cosmopolitan experience.

At the beginning of the eighties, the motherly McDonald's had a fleeting French affair. France's tradition of gourmet food probably did not make it seem likely to be one of the most attractive lead-countries in the company's European advance. So the business in Paris was licensed to a single franchisee. The McDonald's fast food concept quickly proved itself to be just as welcome with busy Parisian families as other Europeans. Unfortunately, McDonald's franchisee, flushed with the success of the business, was equally tempted to choose such prime take-away sites as a shopping arcade dominated by St Lazare's pornographic movie house as he was to select respected boulevards for all the family. McDonald's soon had to buy back the franchise.

This fable illustrates that a would-be global enterprise has to operate a continuing balance between the commitment to its core beliefs and the more expedient practices of local marketing.

Whatever the source of a business idea, those intent on branding global identities should do a lot of heart-searching as early as possible, not only to convince themselves of their solid competitive foundations, but also to make global gross error-checks on such matters as the hundreds of linguistic interpretations that will be made of their name.

A time comes when a brand which has made an encouraging start in one country needs to test whether it can successfully transplant its imagery in another country. Research using a reasonable sample size ($n = 200$), can give a clear understanding of the marketing task which lies ahead. Usually, this research should be used to forecast which one of three routes is best:

- The brand's excellence as a global concept is strong enough. If so, only relatively minor local customization is immediately necessary.

- Optimization of the brand can achieve a reasonable local business, but changes to the brand mix need to be extensive. Any such changes will need to be balanced against some compromises of the brand's global character.

- The brand cannot expect to achieve a reasonable business at this time. If so, ask for explanations of future trends which should be monitored if the brand's time is yet to come.

Experience has taught me that almost all successful international brands proceed in a new country with research which first tests a faithful translation of the intended global concept. Later this can be carefully and locally customized. This works better than allowing local marketers to design their own understanding of a global concept from scratch.

The first test of a global hunch should always be driven from the company's centre. This gives local marketers the opportunity to feel why the company has a lively enthusiasm for the brand. It also helps the centre to learn directly about local biases in the most relevant way: to learn where there are real conflicts with the corporate or product image which is the company's own transnational ideal. One of the main benefits of market research should be specifically as a communications process between a company's central and local offices.

On one occasion, I was reporting the results of a local test of a would-be global brand which had a track record of success in 12 countries, in terms of both the way it had researched and the business it had quickly gained in each country. My forecast had to be unambiguous: the global concept, as it stood, had no chance of developing any significant business in the local market. I knew that I would need convincing diagnostics for both the local client's office (which had commissioned the research) and their head office (which was naturally a partisan supporter of the brand).

Figure 7.7 illustrates one of the key diagrams in my report. Our teenage interviewees understood the brand's pre-use promise of its sexy image, to a similar extent as had teenagers in the 12 countries where the brand was doing good business. However,

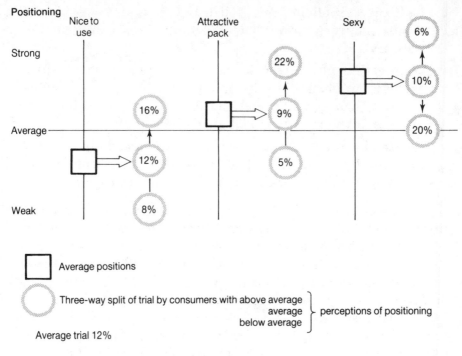

Figure 7.7 Locating the right positioning to trigger trial purchasing of a new brand.

the brand was inducing abysmal trial-purchasing rates, because its sexy image was the opposite of a unique selling point. It was a stand-off. The stronger the recognition of sexy image, the less likely our interviewees were to try buying the brand.

When a market's consumers have very different purchasing motivations from one country to another, the first place to look for clues is the market's eternal triangle of: purchasers ↔ consumers ↔ witnesses. This test brand was clearly designed on the assumption that it would be bought by teenage women for their own consumption as a product which would impress their male friends.

The local market was different. The traditional age for marriage was 25. Until they were 25 years old, respectable girls mixed only with their female peers. The brand's flaunty style was an irrelevance bordering on an embarrassment. What teenage women strongly desired was something delicately pretty that might impress members of their girlish groups. A beautifully packaged brand, as Figure 7.7 intimated, was one of the symbols with a lot of kudos in their witnessing circles.

A lot of this may sound like bread-and-butter stuff which any local marketer should know. But the point was that by demonstrating the impact of the local culture on the company's brand, the brand's champions at the company's centre could adjust their transnational plans. They quickly realized that consumers in other countries in the region would receive the brand coolly for similar reasons. As the brand's packaging identity was not a big feature in its established markets, developing a beautiful flagship pack for the range was still a global option. They set out on their way to developing a global brand 'with multiple entry points' (that is, one brand possessing multiple leading faces for targeting different regional cultures around the world).

PUTTING CREATIVE INPUTS BACK INTO QUANTITATIVE RESEARCH

A brand mix, as the integrated whole that is perceived by consumers, comprises such various parts as the product's functional purpose, the product's cosmetic looks (such as product colour), the product's packaging, its identifying badges (names, logos) and the product's advertising. All of these need to evolve competitively over time and in ways which befit each other. Together, the branding opportunity is to impress with a holistic character; in separation, the risk is a presentation that resembles multiple schizophrenia.

The sources for most of these creative inputs tend to be the personal commitments of various groups of experts, internal and external, to the company which owns the brand. Ideally, market-research projects ought to facilitate communal get-togethers of the brand's creative juices. In practice, things do not always work out that way.

Two dangers in the brand-development process are that creative teams may turn defensive about their own contributions, and that market research may become a piggy-in-the-middle poor relation. This situation is in the breeding when you see every creative group picking out the research findings which they like, and picking on the validity of those they do not. A marketer has to be as tactful with prima donnas as a producer of a Hollywood movie, with the twist that a brand's show requires continuous renewal.

Some professional groups are too jealous of their individual skills. Market researchers indulge too often in almost ritual conflicts between qualitative and quantitative practitioners. Their self-styled tug-of-war between the inspirations that psychologists draw from 'in-depths' with consumers, and the objectivity that only 'large' samples can bring, is actually an example of pushing on a piece of string. Nearly all profitable marketing decisions rely on a fusion of quantitative and qualitative thinking.

Let me provide an example of a research technique which can only work when qualitative and quantitative researchers marry their talents, and when marketers encourage their advertising agencies to feel open-minded about experiments with symbolism.

One day I was called into a meeting with a marketing director who was one of our consultancy firm's longest standing clients. He gave me a memorandum which clearly stated that our research diagnostics were missing out on a whole dimension of branded personality. My attention was drawn to the central paragraph which read as follows:

> We need to generate a set of attitudes/attributes which represent basic market motivations and values, which can be codified such that markets, brands and ideas/concepts can be measured against them, the output being a description that a copy writer can take and interpret in one of a million ways!

I asked for an example. I was told of a cosmetic brand which my client had recently developed with great success. As a counterpoint to the glitzy film-star image that was prevalent among most competitive brands, my client had determined that his brand would be developed in every way like the girl-next-door. In particular, the brand's advertising projected this image, the brand was dressed in packaging which stood out with this personality and the product's distinguishing qualities were absolutely in character. I had to admit that our modelling systems did not include a proper way of monitoring how human the consumers' relationships with particular brands had become.

Over the next few weeks, I met with a variety of experts. Several proposed quite fancy and costly research schemes to attack this problem. I became struck by a different idea. I went back to my client with the proposition that if his marketing team and copy writers would come up with a list of alternative female stereotypes which might occur in the brand's marketplace, then I would construct a quick and simple way of adding appropriate data collection at the end of any consumer interview.

My client and I had converged on the same intuitive logic. If the brand owned such a strong personality, then it would be straightforward for consumers to identify it from a choice of female stereotypes. What we needed was the simplest possible data-collection device to see if the brand was differentiated in this way. If we found that a significant number of consumers were making this identification, then we could cross-analyse their responses with purchasing patterns monitored earlier in the questionnaire. We could then see whether those who identified our brand as 'the girl-next-door' were more loyal purchasers of the brand than those who did not feel this message.

The way we collected our data on female stereotypes is illustrated in Figure 7.8. To our delight 60% of consumers perceived

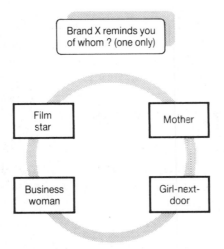

Figure 7.8 Clocking up a brand's persona.

our brand as the girl-next-door, and those who experienced this rapport were by far the most loyal users of our brand. In contrast, most of the competitive brands had less clear identities: the typical brand received 45% mentions as a film star, and none was significantly girl-next-door in character.

For my client, this was the beginning of a system which could support any branding move he might make. Whenever he considered a change to the brand mix or the introduction of a line extension, our female stereotype 'clock' was part of his research questionnaire. It could be used to evaluate whether the brand's overall character was being consolidated or diluted.

The clock method of data collection is the simplest way of experimenting with symbols, stereotypes and roles which brands may build into their character. An individual clock can go through an experimental stage until a standard version is decided on. Subsequently, a standard clock provides the marketer with a monitoring device which supports coordination of a brand's extensions across the world. Examples of clock themes which have been tested internationally are:

- Colours
- Male stereotypes
- Natural elements
- Animals
- Sporting stereotypes
- Seasons
- Female stereotypes
- National stereotypes
- Jewels
- Logo prototypes

In line with my client's original memorandum, clocks provide a flexible measurement-tool so that analysis can reveal associations of images which are made from one medium to another. As Figure 7.9 shows, we can clock up links in images between symbols, brands, markets, lifestyle aspirations and even types of people. Imagery associations made can also be translated from one country to another.

The following case study presented to a conference of European researchers illustrates a fairly sophisticated use of clocks. In this case, the girl-next-door was not a significant player in the marketplace.

> Our client was cultivating the dominant brand (OURS 70% share) in a small but visible product category with the strategic aim of

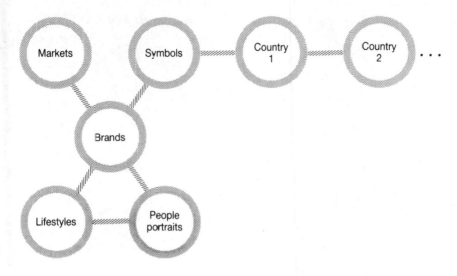

Figure 7.9 Clocking up links in images.

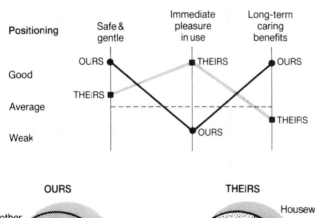

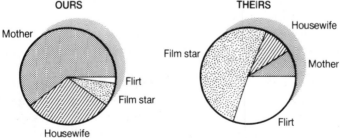

Figure 7.10 How a rival threatened to change the image of OUR market.

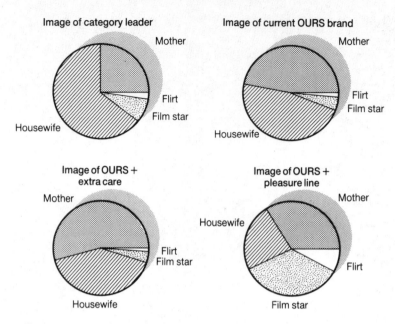

Figure 7.11 Clocking up symbolism for OURS in future target market.

adopting its imagery for future businesses in other much larger product categories. The appearance of a rival brand THEIRS posed a serious threat which models forecast would reduce OURS' share to 45%. Figure 7.10 maps the benefits of both brands and clocks up their extreme contrasts in female stereotyping.

In order to protect his brand, our client prepared two concepts for line extending in the brand's original market. One concept offered an "extra" care positioning as a further consolidation of the brand's USP, while the other concept offered a line attacking the rival's "pleasure sensation" values. Forecasts from simulated testing showed that either concept would retrieve most of our client's original business:

OURS + Extra care: 65%   OURS + Pleasure line: 68%

Ultimately, our client's decision was not based on this information alone but also on projections of the brand's image among consumers which were the principal target of future businesses.

Our client's creative experts concentrated on the clocks shown in Figure 7.11. They had every confidence that "mother" and "housewife" were compatible images for future offensive marketing. In contrast, a diluted symbolism stretching into a film star stereotyping would seriously weaken the heritage credentials for which the brand had been cultivated. Extra care "roots" befitted the evolution of this brand's heritage.

The Power of Analogies

Most branding decisions draw on three guiding spirits:

- A personally inspired sense of direction.
- Market research experiments designed by craftsmen whose motive is to test for practical directions. Be careful not to employ researchers who regard themselves as managers of number factories whose business it is to sell theoretical precision. The choice of market research philosophy, as Professor Lodish has dubbed it, is 'to be vaguely right or precisely wrong'.
- A corporate culture which fosters an encyclopaedic curiosity for marketing analogies.

Branding is an empirical science. Few of its opportunities and risks are entirely new. Marketing analogies offer a method of communicating before tense decisions need to be made. Hindsights from marketing history can help to depersonalize decision-making, and mitigate the tendency to 'speak up for my own department' which confronts any business team. By debating analogies thoroughly before meeting to assess live strategies for a brand, a business team can assemble with a common ground of intuition, instead of an air of vested interests. In this way, companies can seek to limit the damage from one of branding's biggest loss-makers: compromise by committee.

Where do good marketing analogies come from? Ultimately, marketing-oriented companies should refine their own from the stack of practical case-histories in their marketplaces. Fortunately, marketing analogies can also be swapped. Before accepting or dismissing an analogy, begin by asking whether it raises any interesting questionmarks.

This chapter presents three of my favourite analogies for marketing debates. The ideal way to test each analogy is to choose a corresponding marketing example from your own experience.

When a market leader is defeated

All branders need to act on the special window of opportunity and risk which occurs when a market leader is facing defeat – when it has become clear to consumers that a brand which has had a long-established dominance of a market is being overtaken by another brand. What usually happens next is that the consumers' wants become unstable as the publicly accepted reference point of the market – the image of the old brand leader – starts to be severely questioned.

Most established market-leaders trade on a 'halo effect'. To be seen with the brand leader is to be popularly acknowledged as knowing how to make the most discerning choice. When a market leader faces defeat, the process goes into reverse. Emotional associations which had been linked with the image of the winner can easily turn into signs of the loser.

In Britain, in the late seventies, taxation changes advantageous to large cigarettes overturned the cigarette market. Benson & Hedges' King Size took over from the smaller Players' Number 6 which had dominated the market for years. Players' emotional chord was popularity – the kind of cigarette everyone was happy to share had used such slogans as 'people like you are changing . . . changing to Number 6'. The appeal which Benson & Hedges brought with it on ascension to the throne revolved round snob values such as 'discover gold' an image projected by its packaging. Across the market as a whole a new trend swung into motion: branded status symbols were in, brands with a matey appeal were on their way out. This proved to be a setback from which the popular Players' portfolio of brands – and its then independent parent company Imperial Tobacco – never fully recovered.

Many marketers can recall an isolated but traumatic experience of being a defeated brand leader. Nobody in a company wants to be the first to suggest that the consistently successful premise of their branding may have turned sour. All too often, paralysis of action infiltrates until it is too late to halt the consumer revolution. Competitive branders in the marketplace may also need a lot of courage. Yesterday's research programme, which may be close to fruition after years of development, could be redundant if there is going to be a quantum change in consumers' wants. But, the marketing team, which is constantly on the lookout for the defeated-leader syndrome, can turn the situation to great advantage. While an old leader is facing defeat, and until a new leader draws well clear of its competitors, the window of opportunity is open to all to create the new market in their own image.

The phenomenon of the defeated leader is not one which has received widespread coverage in marketing literature, partly because in structurally mature markets the inertia in favour of the brand leader, of which the halo effect is a part, is so great. An extract from Saatchi & Saatchi's 1984 report (Figure 8.1) demonstrates for how long many brand leaders' traditions have stretched.

Whether all branded markets will be so structurally stable in the nineties is an open question. Post-1992 European markets probably will not be. Everyone involved with the marketing

US brand leader		UK brand leader	
Year 1923 & *Current position*		*Year 1933* & *Current position*	
Campbell's soup	No. 1	Brooke Bond, tea	No. 1
Coca-Cola, soft drinks	No. 1	Cadbury's, chocolate	No. 1
Ever Ready, batteries	No. 1	Colgate, toothpaste	No. 1
Gillette, razors	No. 1	Ever Ready, batteries	No. 1
Gold Medal, flour	No. 1	Gillette, razors	No. 1
Ivory, soap	No. 1	Hoover, vacuum cleaners	No. 1
Kodak, cameras	No. 1	Johnson's, floor polish	No. 1
Life Savers, mint candies	No. 1	Kellogg's, cornflakes	No. 1
Nabisco, bisuits	No. 1	Kodak, film	No. 1
Sherwin Williams, paint	No. 1	Rowntree's, pastilles	No. 1
Singer, sewing machines	No. 1	Schweppes, mixers	No. 1
Wrigley, chewing gum	No. 1	Stork, margarine	No. 1

Figure 8.1 The longevity of brand leaders?

function needs to be on the lookout for future scenarios which may feature a defeated market-leader.

Creating a new market or entering an old one

I first met the concept of marketing to a minimum critical mass in India. My American client was aiming to pioneer the first national market for a type of household cleaner. The logic of his launch planning was quite special. The key point to note in pioneering a new market is that you are aiming to market a whole new habit as well as a brand. An established product-category enjoys the advantage of being on consumers' shopping lists. Against this background, the job for a new brand is to compete against established brands for the consumers' choice. When you pioneer a new market, you first compete to become a habit – a regular shopping item.

In India, the recent growth of network TV was being acclaimed by most marketers as a great boon for national branding, but my client refused to consider its use during the first two years of his launch. This would have jumped the gun by expensively promoting a product before consumers had learned to use it – or even to recognize it. Instead, his launch took the brand to the people, town by town; matching local advertising with sampling, on-street promotions and point-of-sale material. All of these were designed to involve the retailer in being an expert on the product's use. Region by region, the strategy was to develop a critical mass of consumers and retailers, from whose word-of-mouth endorsement of the brand the business would snowball.

On my return from India, I sifted through many case studies on 'pioneers of new markets' including some quite sophisticated examples like the introduction of frozen-food ranges in Japan. The patterns of successes and failures in these activities were fairly clear – and surprising. The *modus operandi* for pioneering a new market can be quite a shock for marketers used to intense

Mature market	Pioneering market
● New brand's sales often stabilize within two years of launch (because awareness, distribution, trial and repeat purchasing stabilize).	● Aim during first two years for minimum critical mass. Sales can then be grown steadily provided you maintain pioneer's lead.
● Launch mechanisms act as intense burst: – mass communications channels – distribution builds up quickly – consumers make fast judgements of the brand	● Plan launch as continuous flow: learning of your brand's benefits among retailers or consumers may be slow. An intense launch may squander a brand's resources before the market is ready for it.
● Effectively brand is quickly put on 'shopping list' – or else forgotten.	● More of launch budget should go on local activities such as point-of-sale promotions designed to make shopping for the brand a habit.
● Habits in using product and word-of-mouth effects diffuse quickly.	● Word-of-mouth effects and 'peer following' evolve over time. Target population often grows naturally.

Figure 8.2 The contrasting challenges of market entry.

launch bursts aimed at gaining quick recognition in mature markets. Figure 8.2 summarizes some contrasts which have prompted some intriguing debates at international marketing conferences.

Corollary: the critical mass of global brands

Consider the ways in which megabrands are pioneering the transnational marketplace. Their minimum critical mass is visibility in a cosmopolitan variety of countries and settings. Once a brand has achieved this, it becomes clear to consumers in other countries that it is an international status symbol; in some sense, their country may be missing out on a special kind of experience. The processes which communicate this include jetsetters' word-of-mouth (the duty-free syndrome) and peer group cultures across countries. They are helped by international televisual programming where the brands happen to be (promoted as) props which the players use. Once a megabrand acquires its critical mass, it can exploit its own kind of transnational teaser campaign.

Compare the way an aspiring megabrand teases its way into the global marketplace, and the way that one brand cultivated its position as one of the first nationals in the United States of America before nationwide marketing became a common practice. These details about the original launch of Camel cigarettes come from Julian Lewis Watkins's book *The 100 Greatest Advertisements*:

> The Cigarette Industry – like so many industries in the early days of the 20th Century – began its development with sectional brands ... After a long time in studying the various sectional brands, Mr Reynolds decided that he had perfected the proper blend for a national cigarette. He bought the name CAMEL from a small independent company in Philadelphia for $2,500.
>
> Market introduction was done by Sales Divisions, of which there were 87 in the United States. Every advertising campaign started off with teaser copy in newspapers, approximately forty inches in size.
>
> The first advertisement was a very simple teaser display – using the words "The Camels Are Coming".
>
> The second advertisement featured the wording "Tomorrow There Will Be More Camels in This Town Than in Asia and Africa Combined."
>
> The third advertisement stated "Camels Are Here" and proceeded to describe the brand.
>
> Camels grew from 4th place to 1st place in five years securing about 40% of the entire cigarette business.
>
> Naturally, competition switched its tactics from sectional sellers to national brands that could compete on a national basis with the success of Camels – and the big cigarette battle got under way.

An early pioneer of interstate kudos.

A set of positioning guidelines

A branded business works continually to renew its public's perceptions. Three guidelines help a balanced positioning strategy to evolve: consistently build on your brand's strength; never make a hasty retreat from a strength; do not become obsessed by your strength. Let us consider these in reverse order.

An obsession with a brand's traditional strengths can cause a company to become blind to the outside world. One notorious example was a leading manufacturer of handyman's tools, whose pride in the brand's offer of a lifetime guarantee went too far. Over the years, increments in the quality of the company's products became a technical obsession. By then its quality boosts were no longer recognizable to the growing DIY fraternity. The company's once-distinguished reputation was translated over the years into products which were out of touch with their marketplace on price and user-friendliness.

Along with price, branders should keep an eye out for five 'in-touch' factors (see Figure 8.3). If a brand fails to recognize consumers' minimum standards on any of these factors, even its most loyal users will increasingly switch to something else.

These factors may seem obvious enough. But as branders compete over far more subtle claims to switch consumers on to their brands, it is easy to lose sight of one of the more basic factors which cause consumers to switch off. One discipline which helps to keep a brand on track is to compare every benefit a brand promises against the 'in-touch' factors. In what ways does it make positive(+), negative(−), or interesting (?) connotations.

- Convenience
- Safety
- Performance
- Consistency
- Social acceptability

Figure 8.3 Losing touch with consumers: five factors to respect.

Convenience

+ wash all temperatures
− handle carefully
? much less product necessary

Safety

− rash (in-use, after-use)
? environment
− caring image

Performance

+ added performance

Consistency

− variation in enzyme composition

Social acceptability

? environment
? modern/scientific image

Figure 8.4 'Is biological': unique selling points need constant retouching.

Figure 8.4 shows a hypothetical audit for the proposition that a detergent powder 'is biological'. Consumers' common-sense interpretations of 'is biological' evolve with events in the marketplace. So the brander of a biological detergent needs to monitor how these associations with the 'in-touch' factors vary over time.

The only occasion when a brander should plan to desert a positioning strength is when consumer wants are irrevocably changing, so that yesterday's strength will be tomorrow's weakness. This was evident in Britain's supermarket scene of the late seventies when store locations moved from competitive town-centre sites to isolated out-of-town superstores. In the space of a few years, the traditional supermarket benefit of being known for the best bargains became a liability, particularly among super-markets' own-label brands. The superstore shopping experience requires a journey to a single location, which involves most shoppers in a round-trip of an hour or more. Opportunities for price comparisons get hidden, and once a superstore habit is adopted a sort of price-unconsciousness sets in. At this point the store's own-label brands take on a new relevance. If they feel inferior in usage, then that may prompt a customer to question whether that particular superstore's ritual is worthwhile. In town, it was street savvy to shop for the best supermarket bargains; out of town, going repetitively to a cheap superstore for the week's groceries is like electing oneself to a bargain-basement lifestyle.

When a brander deserts a positioning strength for no good reason, he practically gives away part of the brand's investment to the competition. Desert a unique strength and a competitor will take it over. There is little chance of getting it back. Previously loyal customers feel hurt by a capricious U-turn in what a brand stands for. Theirs may have been every bit as much a mental investment in the image of the brand as the company's was a financial one. This is why consistency of style is the byword of branding. The marketer who ignores this gets a public pillorying for wasting everyone's resources.

Let us return to the brand's focal point: its unique selling proposition in the three-in-one-sense of product heritage ↔ social statement ↔ emotional heartland. The core strength may be conceptualized narrowly: a strong niche brand may then result. Or the core strength may be cooperatively elected as a spiritual image, with which every public act in the brand's name will aim to link up further connections. Figure 8.5 reflects on the Benetton example of Chapter Two. We can almost feel the enthusiastic leaps the company has made in building its brand's united world of colours.

Product A–B–C

A Colourful clothes
B Colourful shops
C Other colourful flagships
   (for example, perfumes)

Social statements 1–2–3

1 Add some colour to your world
2 Join the brand's colourful clan
3 Vote for multiracial harmony

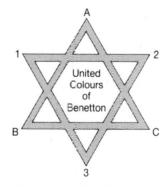

Figure 8.5 Colours: the emotional heartland of Benetton.

The Branded Tree of Life

Can we develop a picture of a world class brand? Like an organization chart, the picture should help people around the world, who were contributing to the brand in its marketplaces, to share a continuous view of their efforts. Healthy growing brands depend on management balancing many kinds of decision. Directions for the evolving business should be the result of a framework which helps monitor a corporate consensus of the global opportunities and risks which confront the brand.

How do the public see the effects created by a company's assemblage of global marketing skills in a brand? In Figure 9.1, I suggest that perceptions of a global brand are rooted in marketing skills which come mainly from seven overlapping compartments.

For a specific brand, the labels for these skills of global marketing should be refined in more detailed lists. The process of comparing priorities which different company managers attach to their world class brand is a valuable organizational exercise. The framework also provides a more general starting point. Good connections between all these compartments of marketing are a necessary condition for an organization to grow as a world class brand. As all these manifestations of the marketing function cost money, they also compete with each other for a balanced share of the capital invested in the brand.

There is no longer a general rule on which investment comes first in the development of a world class brand. While the progress of a market may be measured by the evolution of product excellence, it is a mistake to believe that strong marketing organizations, and their world class brands, necessarily stem from the excellence of their own manufacturing base. Brands as diverse as Nike and Harrods are proving that expert merchandis-

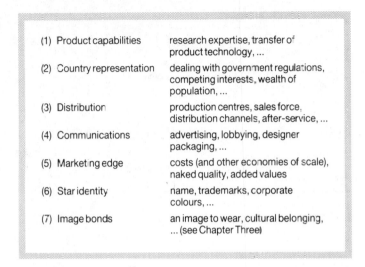

(1) Product capabilities	research expertise, transfer of product technology, ...
(2) Country representation	dealing with government regulations, competing interests, wealth of population, ...
(3) Distribution	production centres, sales force, distribution channels, after-service, ...
(4) Communications	advertising, lobbying, designer packaging, ...
(5) Marketing edge	costs (and other economies of scale), naked quality, added values
(6) Star identity	name, trademarks, corporate colours, ...
(7) Image bonds	an image to wear, cultural belonging, ... (see Chapter Three)

Figure 9.1 Seven sources for marketing brand visibility.

ing of collections of other people's products can be as lively a way of growing a brand as direct manufacture. Other service brands may not involve the manufacture of anything more concrete than ideas consistently implemented.

Marketers working for many of the world's leading manufacturers of fast-moving goods accept the working hypothesis that many of their brands can no longer rely on significant product pluses. From shampoos to toilet soaps, chocolate bars to coffee, many branders rule their markets with parity products – products which, divested of their branding skills, are no better than ones which leading competitors are capable of manufacturing. When marketing textbooks talk about new product development as the lifeblood of all enterprises, world class branders should think of 'product' in a broad sense – that which materializes from directing a valued and unique permutation of skills rooted in all the compartments of global marketing.

As a corporate asset, the world class brand takes on a global worth. When a company elects to assemble global marketing skills under the single banner of a brand, everyone needs to be clear on the strategic choice which is being made. Figure 9.2 illustrates how to begin a checklist of horizons impacting on a brand's function as a mediator of future goodwill. Transnational marketers can no longer afford to concentrate only on

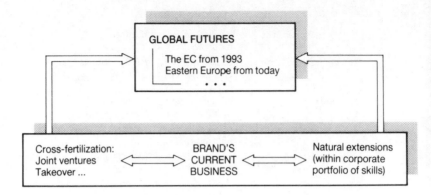

Figure 9.2 Environmental futures of a world class brand.

maximizing a brand's current business in local marketplaces. Much of the brand's worth may now be in its global credentials for future extensions – entries into new countries and product categories and collaborations in new forms of joint ventures. Further coordination is needed to anticipate future environmental scenarios and the likely impact of world class competition.

We do not have a proper picture for the strategic planning of a world class brand until we integrate Figures 9.1 and 9.2. A metaphor may help to keep a unified picture in mind. We can view an individual product line as a tree with roots in its own specific assembly of marketing skills. As the global brand is cultivated the tree becomes a forest. This is how the strategic justification of a world class brand evolves from exploiting the total synergies of the process of global marketing:

> Imagine selling a thousand product lines around the globe under the same name, each drawing on seven overlapping sources of marketing excellence and contributing to corporate worth in three ways. This process is global branding.
>
> Before hyping the branded asset, take heed of an obstinate fact. A global brand's uniform identity is its biggest risk as well as its biggest opportunity. Scandals wreck mega-stars whether branded or human. The branded kind can also be exposed by such simple means as a visibly better competitor.
>
> We may depict a brand as a corporate 'Tree of Life'. Its worth blossoms in three ways: the current business, the credentials for endorsing other products in the corporate portfolio and the

opportunity-costs of cross-fertilisation in other corporate environments. The prospects for future extensions of a brand's image can be worth more than its current business. Conversely, a poorly conceived extension can start a rot from which a brand never recovers.

Recently inflated opportunities of owning today's famous brands stem from forecast changes in the marketing environment. They all point in the direction of globalisation, however slow this may be. These include corporate speculation that 1992 will signal the dawn of a triad of mega-marketplaces (Europe's, America's and Asia's (led by Japan)), the technology for international media (eg satellite broadcasting), and the suspicion that people everywhere as consumers may share more common bonds than the nationalistic boundaries of the twentieth century have so far recognised.

A brand's power as an agent of perpetual fashion takes root in seven kinds of marketing skills: product capabilities, national representations, distribution links, media employed, operational edge, famous identity, image-bonds. Above all, management of a global brand is an exercise in continuity of style.

As brands feed on different priorities of skills, they configure their companies' roots of marketing excellence. This is one reason why intended takeover synergies often fail to materialise, and conglomerates then become worth less than the sum of their parts.

Profitable corporate forestry of brand portfolios has always relied on boardroom photosynthesis. Today's difference is that a global brand can be as vulnerable as its biggest weakness. It should be directed to combine states of competitive excellence and adequacy in current markets and on all future scenarios. Even the largest transnational company can only expect to manage a handful of global brands. Like subdivisions of a corporation, global brand and company survival tend to become natural reciprocals.

Figure 9.3 illustrates the integrated nature of the process of World Class Branding.

(On-Hand Communications Ltd)

As a planning tool the 'Tree' has the advantage that managers may debate strategies prompted by its parts, while its systematic framework keeps the overall perspective in sight. We can illustrate this by posing some of the questions which different parts of the tree stimulate and by discussing some corresponding examples.

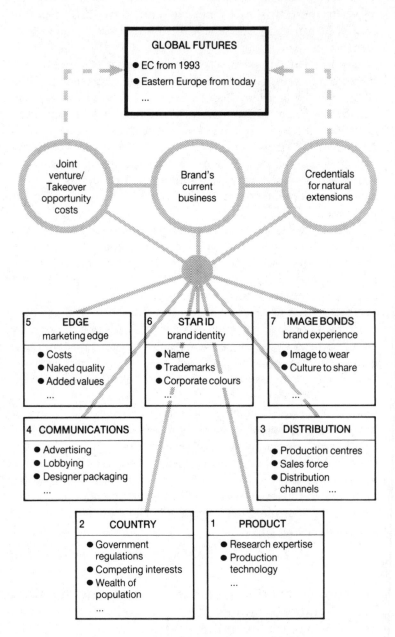

Figure 9.3 The branded tree of life.

Root issues

In which roots do the biggest corporate investments lie and on what scenarios do these become vulnerable? In which roots are the keys to the brand's public image and how can these keys be reinforced across international frontiers? How will the driving forces of the brand vary at different cycles of its evolution between entry into a market and brand maturity?

EXAMPLE WHAT ARE THE DIFFERENT DRIVING FORCES BETWEEN SONY, COCA-COLA AND LACOSTE?

All of these brands rely on a complete mix of global marketing skills, but at the same time the most critical factors affecting the brands' standings with consumers seem to be very different.

Sony is a 'product' company renowned for manufacturing electronic goods that have state-of-the-art reliability. The purpose and the burden of being Sony is that its R & D team must keep on delivering products which pioneer their markets, while established product lines must maintain the Sony standard of quality at production sites around the world.

Coca-Cola's global presence relies on its visible imagery and its distribution force. Divested of its imagery, taste tests between colas prove to be very confusing (with preference for the Real Thing being far from assured). But the brand's visible expression of its social acceptability and total distributional impact leave the rest of the branded world trailing in its wake. According to the Landor ImagePower survey, in 1988 Coca-Cola was the most powerful brand in the world, outshining over 2000 brand names. The remainder of the top 10 were: (2) IBM, (3) Sony, (4) Porsche, (5) McDonald's, (6) Disney, (7) Honda, (8) Toyota, (9) BMW and (10) Volkswagen. (A follow-up survey in 1990 served to confirm Coca-Cola's lead. In this survey Mercedes-Benz, Kodak, Nestlé and Pepsi-Cola made the top 10 nudging out Porsche, Volkswagen, Honda and BMW.)

The apex of Lacoste is the identity invested in the sign of the alligator. The force of this brand stems from the unique

1stLandorImagePowerSurvey™

World's Top Ten Corporate and Brand Names

In an image power study to evaluate both recognition and respect/esteem, 10 corporate and consumer brand names emerged as winners. The survey was worldwide, carried out in Europe, Japan and the USA.

1. Coca-Cola

6. Disney

IBM

2. IBM

HONDA Ⓗ

7. Honda

SONY®

3. Sony

TOYOTA

8. Toyota

4. Porsche

9. BMW

5. McDonald's

10. Volkswagen

1stLandorImagePowerSurvey™
L A N D O R   A S S O C I A T E S
3 Hill Street, Berkeley Square, London W1X 7FA Tel: 01-409 0722
London San Francisco New York Tokyo Hong Kong

Ten world powers and their logos.

visibility of this symbol, broadcast far and wide by the chests of the famous.

Natural extension policies (corporation's own resources)

What extensions to the brand (across countries and product categories) should the company consider? How would each extension support itself and the megabrand? What are the dangers of the brand over-extending itself? . . .

EXAMPLE: OVER-EXTENDING?

Here is how Deirdre Fernand and Margaret Park of *The Sunday Times* reported why 1989 became the first loss-making year for Laura Ashley:

> A year ago it would have seemed inconceivable that the Laura Ashley group, purveyor of sprigged cotton to the middle classes for more than 30 years could come unstitched so spectacularly.
>
> But as the company that brought us Victorian milkmaid dresses and navy gabardine mid-calf skirts was rubbing its bruises, rumours of poor management, tired image and time-warp products were abounding. Kimlan Cook, a City analyst who has studied the company, summed it up last week: "Laura Ashley seems to have lost its way in terms of style and is failing to win new customers".
>
> That view is echoed by Jocasta Innes, author and design consultant, "You feel that their finger has dropped off the pulse," she says. "You don't rush to their shops to see what they are doing." She believes the crucial mistake was the company's introduction of furniture and an upmarket, more expensive "drawing room" look.
>
> "They blew their image. If they had stuck to the inexpensive country cottage look, they might have been all right. In the Eighties they just got too grand and expensive."
>
> A sad epitaph, indeed, for the even sadder story of Laura Ashley herself – the woman who made such an impact on fashion and furnishings, and who died in an accident just over four years ago.
> . . .

At its height in the Seventies and early Eighties, Laura Ashley was the byword for a particular nostalgic lifestyle – a lifestyle that you could buy in a dark green bag at any of 180 shops around the world. She was the Ralph Lauren of Britain, selling the epitome of Englishness and traditional values. The look was country cottage and it was cheap; moreover – and in this, perhaps, lay the seeds of its downfall – it was instantly recognisable.

In the Sixties the silhouette with its floppy hats, flowing skirts and scooped necklines was inspired by the arrival of flower power; the Seventies saw the advent of white high-necked blouses with leg-of-mutton sleeves and ruffles; by the Eighties, not only strapless taffeta ballgowns but also taffeta jodhpurs had been introduced; and by 1990 Laura Ashley encompassed an entire life kit – wall-paper, soap, perfume, curtains, paint, iron bedsteads, crystal, copper saucepans, ceramic tiles, china, bedroom screens, *chaise longues*, scalloped blinds, tapestry cushions, mirrors – and the perennial hats.

Critics, such as a former design director of the company, say the group grew up too fast. It seemed that at one moment it was a small family firm. The next it was a chain store. The company started to lose its personality when it went public.

A good brand which becomes top heavy is a sad sight – let alone a great one like Laura Ashley with a worldwide audience. While we can hope that Laura Ashley (with new support from Japanese investors) will manage to recover, it is clear that the lure of international marketplaces will increasingly cause some spectacular failures among youthful businesses which overreach themselves. Paradoxically, like Laura Ashley, these will often be strongly differentiated brands with little direct competition. They will be failures, not of the original business concept, but of an organization whose management unilaterally tries to take on too many of the skills of global marketing, too fast. These occurrences will not be a denial of the strategic benefits of global branding, though some commentators will say so. The dangers of over-extending are already well chronicled in local marketplaces. While hindsight makes it easy to make carping remarks, Laura Ashley, since its founder's death, has compounded many of the classical risks of over-extending. It is worth noting them here:

- Extending a popular brand upmarket is rarely a profitable

manoeuvre. (Exceptions are sometimes found when a consistent strategy is steadily implemented over the long term.)

- Laura Ashley's image strikes a chord with the past which touches a wide public – the source for an occasional souvenir rather than a kit for orchestrating a total lifestyle.

- Laura Ashley was a world class designer. Most of the new lines which she brought out were newsworthy. More than that, they added a vibrancy to a rotating range of goods – history always had a contemporary edge while it was in Laura's hands.

- Geared up as a public company, the business seems to have raced forward in all directions open to the global marketer, from manufacturing of products outside its traditional capabilities, to a major investment in chain stores. Instead of establishing strong local partnerships, the company bore most of this expansionary burden on its own. Business areas which should have been at the experimental periphery suddenly became the centre-pieces distracting management's attention from the skills it knew best.

Brand cross-fertilization (alliances and external resources)

What joint venture or takeover extensions to the brand would be valuable and to whom? Which roots are at a just-in-time premium? . . .

EXAMPLE: LOCAL MARRIAGES

Skilful flexibility in licensing and franchising will be fundamental to the development of many global brands over the next decade. This is the way to enjoy the dual benefits of world fame and local enterprise. In different ways Benetton, McDonald's, The Body Shop and Hilton Hotels illustrate the principle. Among traditional manufacturers, innovators like Cadbury Schweppes had earmarked this as a leading avenue towards European branding 10 years before the starting guns of 1993. Witness how the company paved its way to Italy:

> Italians consume soft drinks with a fervour that they normally reserve for pasta. But with over 400,000 retail outlets, the market is very fragmented. High distribution costs – further inflated by the elongated lie of the land – mean vast quantities must be sold to achieve healthy profit levels.
>
> This represented a major problem for the premium priced but low volume Cadbury Schweppes range of mixers. For profitable operations a new and viable alternative had to be found to the traditional manufacturing approach. So in 1983 Cadbury Schweppes entered into a highly innovative partnership.
>
> The chosen partner was San Benedetto in Scorze, near Venice, the proud possessor of the largest soft drinks factory in the world. This state-of-the-art industrial site is capable of a herculean output of more than 600m litres a year.
>
> Employing this one colossus, as opposed to a few standard sites, would ordinarily result in huge distribution problems. Not for these Venetians. They overcame this by shrewdly distributing through a network of wholesalers.
>
> This strategy, plus a fixation with driving down manufacturing costs, has led to San Benedetto achieving the enviable position of the lowest cost producer in the Italian market.
>
> The marriage between the companies was no one-sided affair, though. Schweppes' contribution to the union was the portfolio of famous premium brands that San Benedetto lacked. This remarkable Anglo–Italian alliance thereby boasted an organisation and product range to be reckoned with.
>
> The icing on the wedding cake was Schweppes' creation of a range of drinks specifically tailored to the Italian palate: a triumvirate of Tropical Dry, Lemon Dry and Grapefruit Dry.
>
> (*Cadbury Schweppes Brochure*)

Environmental forestry

How will the brand be affected by alternative future scenarios on competitive or environmental changes? Has the brand pre-empted an international position? Are competitors for this

position product-led (that is, in the same industry) or commu-
nications-led (that is, potentially from other industries)? Which
are the brand's flagship lines, among which audiences and on
what visible occasions? How will the brand's identity exploit
international convergence in communications media, distribution channels and PR league tables (that is, being number one in
what)? What are the brand's most vulnerable points for competitive attack, or accidental loss of consumer confidence? . . .

EXAMPLE: EUROPE'S TEST MARKET FOR SEMI-GLOBAL BRANDING

1992 will not change the European consumer (much), but it has
already changed the ways that leading companies see their businesses. Branders who were until quite recently instructed to
target on every national difference are now searching for every
European commonality. Ian Fraser of *The Independent on
Sunday* provides some examples of the changing commercial
philosophy:

> Before the takeover of Distillers by Guinness, famous brands such
> as Johnnie Walker and Dewars were marketed by different local
> distributors in each country. They had free rein to do more or less
> what they chose, which resulted in a wasteful patchwork of posi-
> tionings with 50 different campaigns for Johnnie Walker alone.
>
> Guinness was motivated by a desire to inject some of its legen-
> dary marketing genius into these brands, which lacked any cohe-
> rent identity after decades of weak management. United Distillers
> has radically overhauled the spirit company's ailing marketing
> operation.
>
> Unable to tolerate inefficiency, United Distillers has won back
> control of the distribution network, either by setting up joint
> ventures or buying its distributors outright.
>
> Phil Parnell, United Distillers' marketing director, explains the
> logic behind the new centralised approach. "While we accept
> there are cultural differences, Europe is becoming more and more
> homogeneous as people move across borders. Consumers'
> attitudes to Scotch whisky don't differ that much from Malaga to
> Stockholm.
>
> Our brand strategies are now uniform right across the Continent.

Creative content is the same with minor local adaptions. This is much more economical and efficient."

. . .

Mike Dowdall, detergents co-ordinator of Unilever said: "An organisational structure based on autonomous national companies means concentrating on the differences that exist in markets rather than the similarities. All too often, a local manager faced with the prospect of an international brand called Bloggo will act on research that tells him that Bingo would be a better name, red would be better than blue, lemon perfume would be better than floral, and so on."

These sorts of mistakes are virtually impossible to iron out at a later date. To make sure they never happen again, Unilever is taking much greater central control, and has set up a new organisation called Lever Europe in Brussels to advise on strategic brand development.

EXAMPLE: A BRANDED ORGANIZATION'S WEAKEST LINKS

Brands of mineral water are one of the rare species of product where manufacturing facilities for a global market virtually have to be sited at a single source. While a brand of mineral water needs the strength of a high-profile image to persuade consumers to pay for transporting its bottles all over the world, routine maintenance at the factory of origin for this apparently low-tech product is potentially one of the brand's weakest links.

Philip Jacobson and Jamie Dettmer of *The Times* record a moral tale:

> February 14 1990: All bottles of Perrier, the French mineral water, are to be withdrawn from sale worldwide after traces of benzene, a solvent which has been linked with cancer, were discovered in supplies of the drink in Britain and several other European countries.
>
> . . .
>
> M Gustave Leven, president of Source Perrier, the French parent company, announced the withdrawal of its famous "designer" water yesterday at a press conference in Paris after the spread of the health scare from the United States, where the contamination was first discovered, to Europe.
>
> The decision to dispose of some 160 million of the distinctive

Indian-club shaped bottles, at an estimated cost of £40 million, was taken despite Perrier's insistence that the "infinitesimal" traces of toxic benzene discovered in supplies did not pose the slightest threat to consumers' health.

Perrier blamed faulty maintenance of the filtration system at its plant in the southern town of Vergeze. As a result, small quantities of benzene, a by-product of the natural gas producing the bubbles, had contaminated the production line.

Perrier's survival as the leading aquatic symbol of a healthy life-style will depend on demonstrating that its benzene nightmare is a non-recurring event. Since the whole mythology of mineral waters depends on the minute goodness of their chemical decompositions, we can imagine what a critical wound actual contamination of a brand's source would be. An *appellation controlée* which is linked with the perception of even a trace of benzene would be a terminal illness for any mineral-water brand. The business moral of this affair is that if you brand yourself as purer than pure, then you have quite an image to live up to.

From the branded tree of life to the veritable forest of a global brand, I make no excuse for the colourful metaphors. If we could choose to post one billboard in the minds of the marketing community it should read: 'the larger the goodwill you brand in a single entity, the more you should care about future environmental scenarios, and foster a corporate vigilance directed at protecting your brand from any momentary aberrations which could prove to be its Achilles' heel.'

World Class Futures –
Achievement And Renewal

Companies with world class aspirations fascinate me. Their leaders are taking on the ultimate communications challenge. With my father Norman Macrae, who was Deputy Editor of *The Economist* (1965–1988), I have had the privilege to discuss with several business leaders their views of their companies' future directions as well as their past strengths. This chapter will present souvenirs of our exchanges with three chairmen who seemed to us to have an uncommon sense of where their companies were calmly going about their world class businesses.

Before we turn to these practitioners of management, one business writer's ideas on managing change make useful reading. In the competitive marketplace, the manager needs to know more than a company's reason for being. The uncommon sense of historic excellence must be balanced against an enthusiasm for the future. Confidence in tradition should come from within the company (insiders looking out). Realism about future scenarios comes from tapping sources external to the company (outsiders looking in). The manager must relish being at this interface, if he is to create that flexibility in business direction which permeates throughout a company so that there is a genuine ambition to lead the market instead of being led by it.

The roots of renewal

After searching for excellence with Tom Peters, Robert Waterman's *The Renewal Factor* confronted business's most dynamic
problem – change. This extract introduces Waterman's philosophy that successful managers welcome every initiative which
contributes to the informed evolution of a company – where the
life of the whole depends on promoting a continuous spirit of
learning between all of the parts.

RENEWAL

In concept at least, we build organisations to meet our needs
as individuals. Our needs – as customers, as employees, as
managers, as shareholders, as citizens. But all too often, quietly
and slowly, and while we're not really watching, we're trapped by
the very thing we built to serve us. Suddenly we find ourselves
enslaved by mindless bureaucracy, by habit, or simply by comfort.
People, the only real sources of renewal, stop trying. Customers
vanish. The best employees lapse into apathy, or vote with their
feet and leave.

The challenge is a tough one and not unique to corporations. We
are commonly trapped by the things we seek: material posses-
sions, fame and glory, the good life. Governments, including
elected ones, often ignore or suppress the will of the governed.
The challenge is never completely solved; it recurs like weeds in
the garden. But the challenge is far from impossible. The essence
of living, really living, is renewal. And the highest expression of
management art is the manager's ability to renew a department,
a division, a company, himself. Without renewal there can be no
excellence.

CAUSES & COMMITMENT

Renewing companies constantly renew their causes in the light of
issues: the major problems and issues that shift with time. They
seem to be able to turn tedious issues into noble causes. With
effort, they do so in ways that enhance the dignity of the people
they employ.

Causes are one thing; commitment is another. Commitment is
not something that emanates from management edict. Instead, it
results from extensive communication and management's ability
to turn grand causes into small actions so that people throughout

the organisation can contribute to the central purpose. But there's a trap in moving from cause to commitment. In taking small steps, people often become more committed than they realise. The business of engendering commitment has to be approached thoughtfully on two dimensions. First, the very commitment that caused renewal at one time can blind a company to the need to renew along different dimensions at another time. Second, management efforts to gain commitment must stem from solid, worthwhile values. Leaders use the same means to gain commitment that others use to manipulate.

TEAMWORK ↔ TRUST ↔ POLITICS ↔ POWER

Renewers constantly use words such as teamwork and trust. They are relentless in fighting office politics and in breaking down the we/they barriers that paralyse action. They are heroic leaders, but not lone rangers: little emphasis on charisma; rather, they are outstanding people, supported by others with complementary skills.

While it seems manifest that those who make change happen are politically skilled and understand the use of power, in a positive sense of that word, still the words themselves – politics, power – are so loaded, so rightfully suspect, that those who are good at politics and power often deny it. And because their denials suggest their ambivalence on the skilled uses of politics and power, they confuse the hell out of the young in their organisations. Unless our management vocabulary is enriched on the good and bad uses of power and politics, vacuums will continue to be created, then filled by idealistic innocents who can't get much done, and by manipulators who get themselves advanced but stand for nothing.

Cadbury Schweppes

We interviewed Sir Adrian Cadbury in April 1989, two months before his retirement as Chairman of Cadbury Schweppes (a post he had held for 14 years).

The eighties were a period of accelerating change in the life of Sir Adrian's company. This stemmed from the management conviction that horizons like Europe's 1992 signalled that an era had already begun which would increasingly benefit companies with a worldwide focus. Several businesses were caringly sold (including Cadbury's food division to a management buyout team) so that Cadbury Schweppes could practice a two-pronged ambition to be in the world's top divisions in confectionery and soft drinks. As famous brands became increasingly fashionable, the company had to employ all its strengths to keep clear of hostile bidmakers who were rumoured to be shimmering for a conquest. Here is our souvenir of Sir Adrian's views on the strengths that the management of Cadbury Schweppes will draw on to keep ahead in the next decade:

THE SCALE OF THINGS

To compete internationally in the nineties, a company cannot really afford to be in the second division of a branded marketplace. Confectionery, for example, now has five world class players: Nestlé, Mars, Cadbury, Hershey and Jacobs Suchard. Being one of the leaders matters. It gives you the credentials to invest in the latest technology, to continue to attract the best teams of people, to deal as an equal with the trade, to be respected for independent corporate values in the joint ventures you enter . . .

A few years ago, Cadbury Schweppes marketed products as diverse as Jeyes disinfectants and Smash instant mashed potato. Our world class commitment has involved concentrating all investments on confectionery and soft drinks. It is hard to sell good businesses, especially when they include the cocoa-based beverages, which were the foundation of great-grandfather's company.

CHAIRMAN'S ROLE

Heads of companies should set down what they feel their companies stand for. The character of a company is important to everyone in it and to those with whom the company does business. Belonging to a consistent company is important in earning a living in today's and tomorrow's competitive markets – nice anxious question from a local manager in Nigeria: "will your retirement affect the share price?"

Profitable growth and advance of the reputation of the Company are the two measurements for judging success over time. A century-old Cadbury message reads: "Our policy in the future as in the past will be: first, the best possible quality – nothing is too good for the public." You could say that the character of the Company depends on this kind of responsibility being acted on as a personal commitment by every individual and unit throughout the Cadbury Schweppes business.

CHANGE

Change is constant – in markets, in ideas, in people and in technology. We need enquiring minds, restlessly searching for new ways of advancing the Company. The responsibility for the development of people is shared, the drive must come from the individual, but the training resources from the Company.

MANAGEMENT AUTONOMY WITHIN A FRAMEWORK

Objectives need to be built from the bottom up, but set from the top down. The responsibility for decisions rests on those people locally appointed to take them, but they must keep everybody affected by them as involved and informed as possible.

A co-ordinated framework integrates a strategic vision for capitalising on the total resources of the Company with ideals which the people of Cadbury Schweppes cherish in conducting business and in contributing to the life of the communities of which we are a part.

ETHICS

Sir Adrian won *Harvard Business Review's* 1986 Ethics in Business Prize for an article which developed the proposition that shelving hard decisions is the least ethical course. The paper's opening parable may also be a word-of-mouth reflection on the character of the Company:

"In 1900 Queen Victoria sent a decorative tin with a bar of chocolate inside to all of her soldiers who were serving in South Africa. These tins still turn up today, a tribute to the collecting instinct. The order faced my grandfather with an ethical dilemma. He owned and ran the second-largest chocolate company in Britain, so he was trying harder and the order meant extra work for the factory. Yet he was deeply and publicly opposed to the Anglo–Boer War.

He resolved the dilemma by accepting the order, but carrying it out at cost. He therefore made no profit out of what he saw as an unjust war, his employees benefited from the additional work, the soldiers received their royal present, and I am still sent the tins . . . His dilemma would have been more acute if he had had to take into account the interests of outside shareholders, many of whom would no doubt have been in favour both of the war and of pro-fiting from it."

PREMIUM TAKE-OVERS

The questions everyone should ask, Sir Adrian suggests, are:

- Who stands to make money from the deal? – often the financial manipulators.

- Where does the money come from? – the company, and often that may be only the first thing which the company loses.

(Selected references *The Character of the Company*, Cadbury Schweppes publication; Ethical managers make their own rules, *Harvard Business Review*, September 1987; *Work and the Future*, Blackett Memorial Lecture 1983; *Company Environment and Social Responsibility*, *The Director's Handbook*, 1976.)

WHY THE WORLD CLASS AMBITION? WHY THE COMPANY AS THE BRAND?

If you are curious about either question, Sir Adrian's words repay a second look. When people in a company feel committed to a quality standard, this is a cause worth labouring for. The company may then grow as a communal symbol of faith, a declaration of independence. However, as transnational marketplaces emerge, the national company or even a continentwide company cannot be sure of its independence. World class economies of scale will tend to work against the company which is neither local nor worldly. It may be bought out or it may progressively have difficulty in dealing as an equal with all of its audiences, from trade deals to recruitment of staff, from investment in state-of-the-art technology to being a partner that is respected as an equal in joint ventures around the world.

If you are prepared to be judged by your quality standard on every product you market, the most consistent way to express this faith is the company as the brand. This strategy brings other benefits. You may promote a double message with every commercial you air – a claim about the product line and a lifestyle statement about the company. The creative leap to make with a corporate brand is to stop thinking of the advertising budget as merely a vehicle for targeting today's consumers. A company that really knows its business has more dialogues to build. A clan-like relationship within the company can be fostered which promotes mutual respect between customers and employees as the company gains the warmth of credit of a good citizen. Even takeover artists have second thoughts, as it is hard to see how to profit from buying up goodwill which is also the core motivation for a company's independence.

Sony

Japan has bred more convincing examples of companies as world class citizens than any other country. This is partly because so much of this country's postwar ambitions were channelled into productive excellence, but it would be trite to dismiss the personal inspirations that leading companies embody merely in this way. Western commentators have too often written off Japanese industry as superb imitators. In doing so, they have been blinded by their own myopia to industrial reality. Of course, when you are re-establishing your industrial base from scratch, as postwar Japan did, there is no point in reinventing the basic ball-bearing. But since the day in 1945 when Emperor Showa rewrote what Japanese pride should be about, Japanese corporations have been stunning innovators wherever a long-term business edge has been within their grasp.

Sony has been one of the most visible corporate leaders of the postwar Japanese way since the day of its foundation in 1946. The spirit of Sony, as portrayed by its co-founder Akio Morita in these authorized extracts from his book *Made in Japan*, looks as evergreen for tomorrow's world as it did in yesterday's.

> ### SONY'S BIRTHMARK
> "If it were possible to establish conditions where persons could become united with a firm spirit of teamwork and exercise to their hearts' desire their technological capacity, then such an organisation could bring untold pleasure and untold benefits." Masaru Ibuka – founding statement for the company – 1946.

A SINGULAR IDENTITY

The name would be our symbol, therefore short, no more than 4 or 5 characters. . . . We wanted a new name that could be recognised anywhere in the world, one that could be pronounced the same in any language.

We made dozens and dozens of tries. . . . One day, we came across the latin word *sonus* meaning sound. The word seemed to have sound in it. Our business was full of sound, so we began to zero in on *sonus*. . . . At that time borrowed English was becoming popular in Japan and bright young talents were called "sonny" or "sonny-boys" – a suitable image for our personnel and "sonny" or "sunny" also sound bright and optimistic. Unfortunately, "Sonny" by itself would give us troubles in Japan because it would be pronounced "sohn-nee" which means to lose money! Why not drop one of the letters and make it "Sony"? That was it!

Our name had the advantage of not meaning anything but "Sony" in any language; it was easy to remember and it carried the connotations we wanted. Because it was written in roman letters, people in many countries could think of it as part of their own language. In Japan, as the roman alphabet became common knowledge, people increasingly recognised our company and product name – at no cost to us.

I have always believed that the company name is the life of an enterprise. It carries responsibility and guarantees the quality of the product.

THE FIRST STEP FOR A WORLD CLASS CITIZEN
1960

Slightly over half of our production was going abroad already and I was struck with the idea that our company had to become a citizen of the world, and a good citizen wherever we did business. I decided to found a company called Sony Corporation of America. . . . Sixteen months later, we offered two million shares of Sony common stock on the US market, but getting there may have been the hardest work I ever had to do. We had to comply with the Japanese Commercial Code, the rules of the Japanese Ministry of Finance and the American Securities and Exchange Commission. It was all new and very strange and complicated.

Fortunately, Prime Minister Hayato Ikeda liked the idea, because he was an internationalist and this would be a first for Japan, a first postwar capital liberalisation.

NEW PRODUCTS

For many years now we have put well over 6 per cent of sales into research and development, and some years as much as 10 per cent. Our plan is to lead the public rather than ask them what kind of products they want. The public does not know what is possible, but we do. So instead of doing a lot of market research, we refine our thinking on a product and its use and try to create a market for it by educating and communicating with the public.

Sony 'firsts' include: transistorized TV sets, video recorders for home use, the Walkman, the compact disc system, the 3.5 inch computer floppy disk. . . .

Reaching out: the climate of change

To feel Sony's story – indeed to relive Japan's story in the second half of the twentieth century – Westerners need to filter through many of their bureaucratic oaths of management. The principles of business writer Bob Heller act as a good guide for those who want to build bridges of the mind towards world class aspects of Oriental corporate cultures.

- The concept of the continuously evolving business isn't customer-led or market-driven – it leads the customer and drives the market. Effective change management insists on getting the right answers to six basic questions: Are you selling the right things? Are you supplying these in the most effective way? And at the lowest cost? Are you as good as or better than your best competitor? Are you tapping the widest possible market? Do you have an edge – a unique selling proposition?
- None of the six questions can be permanently answered with

Yes unless the company is continuously changing and genuinely committed to innovation. That in turn will not be effective unless these six barriers are removed: Red Tape, Lack of funds for innovation, Preoccupation with today at the expense of tomorrow, No innovative thinking, No top management support for innovation, An organisation structure that discourages innovation.

- The task and test of change management is how nearly it removes such barriers and closes the gap between the ideal and the real: which starts from having a clear idea of the ideal, then correctly assessing the reality and then acting to close that gap: the process which is also the model for successful planning and successful product development.

- The most effective change masters are the Japanese, who founded adaptive management on ten tenets (1) Take a long-term view (2) Grow internally (3) Go for the largest attainable and profitable market share (4) Get all the information you can about the business and the markets (5) Follow the leader – and pass him (6) Develop new products and services (7) Compete on everything except price (8) Concentrate on your strengths (9) Build a customer franchise (10) Minimise risk.

- Change leadership rests, like democracy, on consent of the governed, but earns that consent by doing what is right, regardless of the impact of established traditions and the conventional wisdom. The examples of Japan and of great commanders in war confirm the formula: the leader changes the "corporate culture" by personal example, symbolic change, moving rapidly into successful action and observing the ten pillars of leadership: Trust, Teamwork, Atmosphere, Objectives, Clarity, Confidence, Back-up, Performance, Humanity and Competitive Aggression.

- Western style hierarchies, especially those which stress seniority and functional division, are obstacles to effective performance – but firms are now moving slowly towards the ideal of collective individualism. This type of organisation is much more difficult to lead – if the leader seeks to operate in the traditional manner: all over the West, however, the old "order and obey" style is giving way to "advise and consent". That means adopting these self-denying ordinances: Spend your time correctly judging future trends; Leave details of daily operations to the responsible personnel; Insist that they make consensus decisions; Always approve what they ask to be done for short-term tasks.

- The more open, collegiate organisation is bound together by a shared, far-sighted philosophy which will always include getting the best out of people, and doing the best for them as a central preoccupation. This means developing the concept of the business as a learning company, in which the learning is top-down, bottom-up and lateral. It demands the creation of strong teamwork, developing functional talents that support and interact with business units whose own "leaders" have the autonomy and authority necessary to develop their own momentum – and their own true teams.

Carrying world class flags

Today, for a company with various business interests and world class aspirations, the first question of branding is: how many world class brands do we really need to divide up the company's business territories? These 'territorial' divisions should no longer be thought of as primarily geographical. Nowadays, they should represent ranges of products with as few distinct leading images as are really necessary. A subsidiary question to ask is: when is commitment to sole ownership of a world class brand an unnecessary luxury?

The international conglomerate which enters the nineties with hundreds of brands is likely to exit the nineties, if it survives intact, with a handful of world class brands and a few dozen local brands. Among its world class brands, I include semi-global double-barrelled names which will be highlighted in a region by the local name that brought the product to fame. It may also mention international pseudonyms. We will see some brands bearing a globe-like badge displaying the product's American, Asian and European names, as a way of reuniting the goodwill that the company's marketers had previously subdivided when christening the same product with different locally inspired names. Some products which could have shared the same leading image united by a common excellence of style, will be regrouped under a corporate division's 'surname' but will retain their product names as forenames.

As trading barriers between countries come down, many companies will need to face up boldly and frankly to the limits of their resources. Partnerships between equals will make a lot of sense. It is time to dismantle the favourite concept of financiers and taxers alike, that a transnational company should have a single parochial centre.

While the future's happening

Nobody surveys renewal of the business world with more authority than Peter Drucker. In outlining his five trends for the nineties in a turn-of-decade article for *The Economist*, Drucker concluded that these trends are already happening. It is only their full impacts which are yet to come:

- The world economy will be quite different from that businessmen, politicians and economists take for granted. The trend towards reciprocity as a central principle of international economic integration has by now become well-nigh irreversible whether one likes it or not (and I don't). . . . Reciprocity can easily degenerate into protectionism of the worst kind (that's why I dislike it). But it could be fashioned into a powerful tool to expand trade and investment, if – but only if – governments and businessmen act with imagination and courage. . . . In the past whenever a new major economic power appeared, new forms of economic integration followed (eg the multinational which was invented in the middle of the nineteenth century when the United States and Germany first emerged as major economic powers; by 1913 multinationals had come to control as much of the world's industrial output, maybe more, as they do now). Reciprocity is the way, for better or worse, to integrate a modern but proudly non-western country such as Japan into a West-dominated world economy.

- Businesses will integrate themselves into the world economy through alliances; minority participations, joint ventures, research and marketing consortia, partnerships in subsidiaries or in special projects, cross-licensing and so on. The dynamics of economic integration are shifting rapidly to partnerships based neither on the nexus of trade nor on the power nexus of multinational ownership for several reasons:

- Many middle-sized and even small businesses will have to become active in the world economy. To maintain leadership in one developed market, a company increasingly has to have a strong presence in all such markets worldwide. But middle-sized and small companies rarely have the financial or managerial resources to build subsidiaries abroad or acquire them.
- Financially only the Japanese can still afford to go multinational. Their capital costs them around 5% or so. In contrast, European or American companies now pay up to 20% for money.
- The major driving forces behind the trend towards alliances are technology and markets. In the past technologies overlapped little. . . . Today there is hardly any field in which this is still the case. Not even a big company can any longer get from its own research laboratories all, or even most, of the technology it needs. Conversely, a good lab now produces results in many more areas than can interest even a big and diversified company. The need for alliances is greater the faster a technology grows. . . . Markets similarly, are rapidly changing, merging, criss-crossing and overlapping each other. They too are no longer separate and distinct.

- Businesses will undergo more and more radical restructuring in the 1990s than at any time since the corporate organisation first evolved in the 1920s. Businesses tomorrow will follow two new rules. One: to move work where the people are, rather than people to where the work is. Two: to farm out activities that do not offer opportunities for advancement into fairly senior management and professional positions (eg clerical work, maintenance, the medical lab in a hospital) to an outside contractor. The corporation in stockmarket jargon, will be unbundled. . . . Underlying this trend is the growing need for productivity in service work done largely by people without much education or skill. This almost requires that the work be lodged in a separate, outside organisation with its own career ladders. Otherwise, it will be given neither enough attention nor importance to ensure the hard work that is needed not just on quality and training, but on work-study, work-flow and tools. . . . Corporate size will by the end of the 1990s have become a strategic decision. Neither "big is better" nor "small is beautiful" makes much sense.

- The shift of ownership in the large, publicly held corporation to representatives of the employee class – ie pension funds and unit trusts – constitutes a fundamental change in the locus and character of ownership. It is therefore bound to have profound impact, especially on the governance of companies: above all to challenge the doctrine developed since the second world war of the self-perpetuating professional management in the big company; and to raise new questions regarding the accountability and legitimacy of big company management. . . . Hostile takeovers have been one early symptom of this. They work primarily because pension funds are "investors" not "owners" in their legal obligations, their interests and their mentality. The raiders are surely right to assert that a company must be run for performance rather than for the benefit of management. They are, however, surely wrong in defining "performance" as nothing but immediate, short-term gains for shareholders. They are also wrong because immediate stockholder gains do not, as has been amply proven, optimise the creation of wealth. That requires a balance between the short term and the long term, which is precisely what management is supposed to provide and get paid for.

- Rapid changes in international politics and policies, rather than domestic economies, are likely to dominate the 1990s. The lodestar by which the free world has navigated since the late 1940s, the containment of Russia and communism, is becoming redundant because of the policy's very success. The other basic policy of these decades, restoration of a worldwide, market-based economy, has also been singularly successful. But we have no policies yet for the problems these policies have spawned: the all-but-irreversible break-up of the Soviet empire, and the decline of China to the point that it will feature in world affairs because of its weakness and fragility. Besides, new challenges have arisen that are quite different: the environment; terrorism; third-world integration into the world economy; control or elimination of nuclear, chemical and biological weapons; and control of the worldwide pollution of the arms race altogether. They all require concerted, common, transnational action, for which there are few precedents. . . . Political life since 1945 has been dominated by domestic economic concerns such as unemployment, inflation or nationalisation/ privatisation. These issues will not go away. But increasingly international and transnational political issues will tend to upstage them.

It is in a brave new world of communicating, such as Drucker's, that world class brands will be doing their job. Marketers have no need for crystal balls, but they should never apologize for the fact that branding is the business strategy responsible for drawing up the company's future commercial territories of the mind. These territories concern quality levels, perceived through criss-crossing dimensions. I would say three of these have a global pre-eminence:

- *Purpose*   spiritual (that is, image) *and* functional (that is, product excellence).
- *Bonding*   employees (that is, their branded organization's reason for being) *and* customers (that is, their brand's reason for being).
- *Worldliness*   global understanding *and* local appreciation.

Here may be a penultimate definition of a world class brand, to distinguish it from any other. If Drucker's five trends do not apply to the heart of the strategy for branding a business unit, then the brand is a local one – with the sphere of responsibilities which this implies. If a business unit's identity does interact with Drucker's five trends (of reciprocity, alliances, restructuring, ownership and transnational citizenship) then a different test becomes important. The nature of the branding – the validity of its world class impact – will depend, in the ways amplified in this chapter, on everyone who is involved with the company.

I do not believe that it is ever productive for a company to believe that it has become world class. Like learning, the world class label repays those who acknowledge that their actions are in a continuous state of aspiration. Still, certain companies can claim to have had more experience at trying to deal with worldwide issues than others. None more so than the major oil companies on whom this century's global industry (that is, 99?% of production in the history of the world) has been founded. It seemed appropriate to close this chapter with a souvenir from one chief executive with a calm and worldly touch.

Shell

We interviewed Bob Reid in November 1989, six months before his retirement as Chairman of Shell UK (after five years in the post and a lifetime's career at Shell) to become Chairman of British Rail. Under Reid's stewardship Shell entered the nineties as Britain's most admired company in a business executive's poll published in *The Economist*. Here is Reid on Shell.

MANAGING THE ESTATE

For Bob Reid the head office extends to the furthest corners of Shell's UK estate. The trick is to keep executive decision-making in the London headquarters streamlined so that most of the week can be spent on site. When people are risking life and limb for the company, you owe it to them to keep abreast of the latest technological challenges at the detailed human level.

Reid, you sense, is keen to dispel images of oil (and gas) as a glamour business. He gives the credits to those whose actions in production are at the forefront of man's technological and environmental skills.

Geography has dealt Reid two natural sources of confidence. The energy fields in the North Sea mean that the UK's most valuable product now streams forth from his native Scotland. Shell's joint ownership (UK and Dutch) provides a cornerstone to the corporate ethos that short-term profit should not be prioritised over sound ecological principles.

SEAWARD SYMBOLS

Shell men have always held the sea in particular respect. A christening tradition began a hundred years ago with the naming of the company's tankers after sea shells, and continues today as seabirds are chosen to identify new North Sea fields: Auk, Eider, Fulmar, Kittiwake, Osprey, Tern. . . . High-tech has its place only if it is kept within human proportions. So be prepared to meet creatures like the humble mussel contributing to Shell's good housekeeping in the North Sea fields. Around every oil platform, buoys suspending baskets of these shellfish at various depths are employed as nature's own scientific instrument for monitoring the cleanliness of the sea.

VENTURES

Reid budgets up to 10 per cent of his time encouraging venture activities. Shell chooses businesses which are directly related to its existing operations, but does not lend out the company's brand name; it regards the energy business as a big enough responsibility. Within this remit, venture businesses vary from the apparently historic (eg candles) to the state-of-the-art (eg semi-conductor structures based on indium phosphide and gallium arsenide). Shell seems to be most at home in fostering the useful, rather than the fashionable. There is also an energy management business whose expertise is guidance on and installation of systems to reduce energy usage costs. Educated consumption is part of the future of the oil and gas business.

THE INFUSION OF EXPERIENCE

Shell's operating advantage is that its young men attain positions at an early age where they have to show responsibility. It then becomes much easier to pick out the high flyers among them than it is in a corporate headquarters. Reid himself had his first big executive job running operations in Nigeria for Shell, then moved to Thailand. The company's management is technology-based, but served by practical accountancy and marketing controls. The Royal Dutch Group keeps tabs on what is happening, but innovation and technological advances are encouraged all through the Group.

(Selected reference: *Good Neighbours*, Shell UK publication)

ENVOI – AHEAD OF GLOBAL PRIVATISATION

In *Megatrends 2000*, John Naisbitt nominates privatisation as one of his 10 gateway trends to the third millennium. Pioneered from the beginning of the 1980s by Britain's Margaret Thatcher, privatisation has struck a chord with governments in over 100 countries. Here too, Britain's favourite company may prove to be a useful role model which has stood the test of time. It is useful to have an oil explorer and operator whose executives can learn from experience in many countries. Single national oil companies (and indeed uni-national companies in any industry operating in the Interlinked Economy perceived by Ken Ohmae) never attain the same level of competitive knowhow, and governments will in future sell them off.

On Ownership

Shell owns one of the most fitting corporate symbolisms of our times. Anyone encountering the Shell logo looks into a mirror which appears to reflect the highest standards that an energy business may aim to achieve. A Shell employee can feel part of a caring corporation as well as an efficient one. He senses his business is rooted in managing a proper balance between exploitation and care of the environment. A member of Shell's global public is confronted with an image which in its nature communicates safety first and is led ultimately to feel that this is the most worldly commitment for an oil company to make.

In the long run, the credibility of the Shell brand – Shell's channel of global communications – depends on living up to the declaration of its identity. Relative to its competitors in the oil industry, Shell has to be seen to be trying harder in exercising care over the environment. The function of the mature world class brand is not simply to target its customers' lifestyles. It frames the standards within which government of the company is expected to operate.

Evolution of a world class brand is a long-term process. Growth depends on integrity of purpose at every level of association between product and image, and depends on every audience which identifies with the brand. As a channel of global communications, the world class brand is a democratic one whose audiences are free to vote against it at any time. This begs a question of ownership: what kinds of company will be best at nurturing world class brands? It looks as if corporate image-makers, once supposed to be shallow, have been doing the deepest thinking on this; while bankers and calculators on the stock exchanges have not.

Ironically, just as the clamour for free markets is being seen to

1900 1904 1909 1930

1948 1955 1961 1971

Where symbol and corporate identity have a common
sense of direction.

be one of the few common aspirations of the Soviet disunion,
such bastions of Western capitalism as the American and British
stockmarkets are losing credibility as environments for anyone
who is serious about investing in the future.

As we saw in Chapter Nine, the Laura Ashley brand of business
was a victim of the expansionary hype which stockmarket flota-
tions too often brought to young companies in the eighties. At
the end of that decade, one of Britain's most astute entrepreneurs, Richard Branson, devoted his energies to steering Virgin
Group back to private status after a brief exposure to City
analysts' business 'planning by quarterly instalments'. Interestingly, Japanese companies are now being welcomed as suitable
investors in Virgin brands. Fujisankei has paid £100 million for
a quarter of Virgin's music division. Seibu Saison (today's owner
of the Intercontinental hotel chain) has taken a 10% stake in
Virgin Atlantic Airways. Branson explains: 'Virgin gets on with
the Japanese because we share common business values. They
are owners and investors for the long term, not punters.'

These words echo the views of Rupert Pennant-Rea whose
survey on capitalism (*The Economist*, 5 May 1990) is convincing
in the thesis that the eighties witnessed too much punter
capitalism. Short-term guessers took over from master-builders
at every level of ownership of Western companies with a stockmarket quotation:

To hold equity in a company is to own part of it: that is a legal axiom which has changed hardly at all in more than 100 years. Behind the legal front, however, the functional reality of equity has been transformed. To shareholders in a typical public company in America or Britain – call it Anglo-Saxon Inc – a share is now little more than a betting slip. It is bought at what a shareholder thinks are good odds, to provide winnings that he hopes will be large. The notion that he owns part of Anglo-Saxon Inc makes as much sense to him that he owns part of Lucky Lady, running in the 2.30 tomorrow afternoon. . . .

   This reality has grown partly because of the growth of institutional investors. . . . There are three questions worth putting to professional money managers in America and Britain. When they buy a slice of Anglo-Saxon Inc, do they think of themselves as part-owner? Or are they placing a bet on tomorrow's race? Or, which is increasingly the case, have they bought the shares only because the company is a constituent of a particular stockmarket index which they are tracking?

   The answers are usually revealing. Few think of themselves as owners, and they tend to be older than the rest. If the trend continues, every one of the next generation of British and American money managers will be punter-capitalists. Yet they usually have good, rational reasons for becoming punters. . . . Even if an institution wanted to influence the long-term, it couldn't. The standard arrangements for exercising influence in Anglo-Saxon Inc – attending annual meetings, voting on resolutions put before shareholders – are simply too weak and the incentive to use them too small.

The eighties have therefore provided startling vindication for concerns relating to the nature of boardroom management aired by Adam Smith over 200 years ago:

The directors . . . being the managers of other people's money than of their own, it cannot be well expected that they should watch over it with the same anxious vigilance which the partners in a private co-partnery frequently watch over their own.

Perhaps the 1988 payment of $56 million to Mr Ross Johnson, former boss of RJR Nabisco, can be called the summit of Adam Smith's misgivings. This record severance payment was made to 'the man who bet the company and lost' as International Management fittingly titled its review of the book *Barbarians at the Gate*. The review went on to paint a picture of a corporation which had lost all sense of its identity:

> Johnson was unique in the way his personality divided. He was half numbers, half arrested adolescent.
>
> The late night frivolity with his top management team as he leap-frogged through the business world makes amusing anecdotal material, but undoubtedly would have appalled the shareholders had they been aware. He loved company-owned apartments, the fleet of jets called the RJR air force, exorbitant compensation packages, and the key to this drama, golden parachutes (he could not lose, no matter what happened).
>
> The rough language alone in this circle is dismaying. The vicious infighting, duplicity and name-calling are features of everyday life. The internal memos and graffiti are witty but bitter. As one RJR executive wrote in a private spoof mini-biography of Johnson: "It all started with a small lemonade stand in Manitoba. The next thing I knew I had sold my mother. The rest was easy."

When corporate behaviour reflects such an immature appreciation of goodwill and its custodianship, anyone connected with the company – whether customer, employee or shareholder – becomes a long-term loser. The nineties are likely to wipe out such businesses. Just when the emergence of transnational markets promises the biggest opportunities to companies which differentiate their purposes in long-term branded positions, many once-famous marketing companies have become the puppets of short-term players.

A world class brand is a communications channel which shares the standards of a transnational business democratically with all its audiences. The most natural level for world class branding is an entire company, because much of the human appeal of the brand then comes from the people who work the business. The typical ownership base is likely to veer away from punter capitalists. As we enter the new millennium, winning companies are likely to be exponents of the Japanese proprietorial style; or rooted in the ethics of the Western family firm; or new sorts of cooperative firm where the seeds of business growth are franchised equitably; or indeed any sorts of foundation which pursue a competitive intent of purpose while seeing profits as the means to but not the end of the mission.

The Japanese have a particular zest as world class branders because after the Second World War they elected to invest as much in corporate pride as they do in national pride. The Honda man is far more dispirited if a Honda product fails to live up to specifications than if Japan fails to qualify for the World Cup.

Is there now any good reason why a brand of nation merits a higher degree of human loyalty than a brand of transnational company? Not surely for those who believe in a United States of Europe. Perhaps the nation and the transnational company should be perceived as related artefacts: communications channels of the most rich and complex kind. The breadth and depth of their operational infrastructures, and the human loyalty which they command as rallying forces of human identification, are predicated by their integrity of purpose and their efficiency in competitive exchanges with the global marketplace. At the end of the day, no institution can be the centre of global goodwill unless it is seen to be accountable for branding the lifestyles of all of its publics.

Brands figure among today's most valuable property rights. World leaders like Coca-Cola have emerged in valuers' books as multi-billion dollar assets.

But if relatively small communities in companies can build such valuable global properties, how much greater is the potential of the branded nation?

Nations that wish to compete effectively on the world stage can learn from corporate PR. Competitive advantage depends on management of your image, reflecting the positive commitments that are the reason for owning a separate identity. Without active cultivation, your identity is prone to negative stereotyping by your audiences and the media, with a little prompting from your competitors.

As the world's markets converge, the strategic purposes of rallying to a national identity are changing. Why do other nations need yours as a partner? What values of independence are mirrored through everyone's perceptions of belonging to a nation state?

Although our televised era of the image for universal consumption is only a few decades old, we may glimpse how winning nations have cultivated goodwill in a worldly manner.

In the space of a generation, Japan's industry has been built on state-of-the-art reliability. Its exports gain from the added value of this global guarantee. Japan's people appear to face up to this image as a matter of the highest honour.

From the early days of Hollywood, the US has enjoyed being host to most of the world's televisual images. One story goes that the people of Dallas found it only natural to invest in a TV series; the town where John F Kennedy was shot was not a glamorous image to live with.

France has done the most to promote the European Community as a European stage and owns a founder's right as a mediator of the single market. We cannot afford to sneer at the rumour that branders are employed by France's ministry of trade to give advice on the style that is expected of the export label *fabrication française*.

Whether you subscribe to the bottom-up concept of brand stretching or the top-down concept of linkages to the corporate identity, the branded way of realising more than the sum of your parts is to harness products and images so that each leads the other. World Class brands, like Disney, take the step a stage further. They aim to own a global forum of visibility which is sufficiently attractive that business partners, including governments, line up to join their club.

Under the World Class umbrella, companies are positioning brand hierarchies to offer the consumers the best of both emotions: worldly discernment and local empathy. The national challenge may present similar opportunities and risks in the marketing of regions and cities.

(*Marketing Week*, 7 September 1990)

Curtain Call

So what ultimately is the point of any brand, let alone a world class one? Advisedly, it is to communicate the direction of a sense of excellence as broadly as it will be humanly needed.

A brand's direction should act like a magnetic force. At the core is the brand's strength. Around this are connected an evolving system of products – both physical ones and spiritual ones.

Like any word, a brand escorts you to its destination. What do you think of when I say French or Italian or American or Japanese or British? Or Chanel or Ferrari or Coca-Cola or Sony or Harrods? What association comes first to mind? What associations come next? How much depth do the associations have? How much personal rapport? Would you expect other people to make similar associations?

So, world class brands enter into a universal language. When such a brand does its job properly, it should prove to be a vital companion to the human imagination, making connections between people as well as referring to them personally. Because we elect the brands we choose to deal with, a brand's style-rules become fashioned in our own images and vice versa.

We should not underestimate the brand's role as an interpersonal mediator; its power as a non-verbal communicator. This grows out of a common awareness of a brand's style – its in-built script which promotions have repeatedly rehearsed in front of a global public. As a result, brands become props in everyday relationships. They make discreet social statements on our behalves. This is often a conscious process as well as a surreal one. Public speakers have always used clothes to create an initial impression with a strange audience. Today, non-verbal languages of first impressions – and the images we proceed to wear

– are variously available for mass participation in the brands which we buy.

Like all leaders of people, a great brand appears to thrive on a combination of heart and soul. The heart is emotional ambiguity, the soul is reassuring constancy. Careful interweaving of these contrasting threads helps to perpetuate a brand as part of the fabric of life.

A world class brand is also an organizational state of being. It represents the particular interests, expertise and resources of a company. The government of the brand involves all the balances of self-interest which this phrase implies. So a brand's style-rules also evoke work-styles and indeed styles of governing.

The constitutions of world class brands are pioneering ones. Their global consumer electorates possess none of the homogeneity which is due to a geographical territory. Instead the electorate's homogeneity stems from what the brand has created. If Disney's Mickey Mouse is the world's most heartwarming representative of family values, let us learn from that rather than 'take the mickey'!

Given that a brand is fundamentally an object of market competition, it can be salutary to use the corporate metaphor of 'the branded tree of life' for the process which transforms a successful product line into a veritable forest of products and images, which become the environmental responsibility of the global brand. The singular identity of a global brand is also its biggest risk. The environmental care involved in managing a brand which incorporates a billion dollars of goodwill requires contingent thinking about some of the smallest details of the business. This has to be one of the tangible responsibilities at the centre of a corporation. In a real sense, consumers buy a guarantee from a world class brand which cannot be decentralized from the heart of the business.

Great brands time-travel using self-perpetuating myths as part of their protective clothing. Among employees the difference between boring routine and proud ritual can be wafer-thin. Working with a brand which everyone feels is legendary can make a telling difference. Ideally, the branded legend impresses by mirroring the motivations of customers and company staff.

Brands add worth to products by dealing with the hopes and fears of human aspirations. Whichever views of a brand you share from this chapter (and book), whether as artefacts of the religion of consumerism or interpretors for commercial marketplaces or transnational states (without land of their own), do not dismiss brands as mere intangibles. The obscene spectacle of a billion dollars of goodwill going up in smoke begins whenever managers charged with corporate responsibilities start to wave their hands in this way.

A brand's common sense of direction should be balanced by careful consideration of the sphere of business which a company and its associates can properly expect to endorse. When this has been done with consistency, the brand has served national marketplaces well in the first part of our era of mass communications. As a second episode envelops us with a converging world marketplace, the motivations of world class branders may be about money, but they should also include such productive business aims as interknitting global societies in friendly ways. If they do this, the constructive purposes of world class brands will be deserving partners of our emotions.

A Catalogue of Competitive Advantages

Introduction

My colleagues at The Marketing Consultancy of Coopers &
Lybrand Deloitte have identified a catalogue of competitive
advantages which we associate with brand appreciation in the
nineties. I am grateful to the firm for permission to reproduce
these business precepts. Sidenotes, which I have added, provide
an index to branding practices which have featured in the text of
this book.

BRAND VALUATION AND APPRECIATION

Brand valuation exercises are highlighting just
how often brands now figure as the company's
most valuable property right. It follows that a
company's portfolio of image-assets may be its
most fundamental source of competitive advantage. Our purpose is to preview ideas being considered by marketing companies as part of their
emerging practice of brand appreciation – the top-
down re-examination of a company's portfolio of
brands aimed at changing the rules of the marketing game.

(1) **Transnational brand seeding** *Step 1*: select
discriminating   distribution   channels   to

establish minimum critical mass of international consumers and the brand's cachet.
Step 2: mass communications marketing
once Step 1 has been achieved.

Seeded beginnings	
Recent	Classical
Phileas Fogg	J&B
Aqua Libra	Haute Coutures
Vidal Sassoon	Coca-Cola (1890 – 1910)

(2) **Double-branding** rebuilds corporate brand
hierarchies by developing internationally
recognized brand umbrellas. The ideal of
double-branding is to offer a global aspiration
with a local touch. Corporate added value is
derived from the brand umbrella which
translates business leadership into a unique
social style.

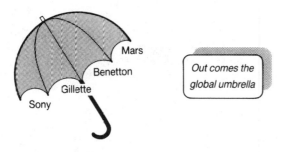

(3) **Over-branded companies** include many
Western fmcg multinationals which are facing the vision of the transnational marketplace with portfolios of hundreds of brands
apiece.

    One solution is to establish a proper bal-
ance between long-term investments (AAA
brands: transnational-unassailable-extend-
ible) and short-term earners (CCC brands:
local-assailable-specific).

    In the long run, brands represent the levels

> *'How many AAA brands can we afford*
> *to invest in ?'*
> *'Is our national brand leader vulnerable to our*
> *competitors global aspirations ?'*

at which an organization chooses to project itself. The advertising budget becomes a fraction of the total organizational investment in a brand as a communications channel. Once geared towards transnational merchandising, the company will not want to market a purely local brand competitively, unless consumers are really willing to pay for its customization.

(4) **The price of quality** Brand leadership depends on presiding over the two consumer sensitivities in a marketplace:

Branding's 1st and 2nd bases 59–62

• the quality standard
• pricing (market price should support the quality image while low-cost planning ensures future margins for manoeuvre)

Value contours 116–19

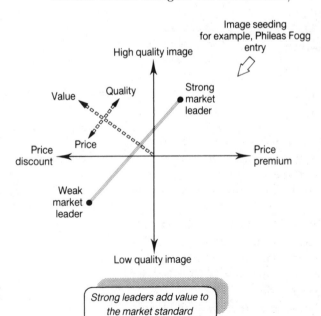

Strong leaders add value to the market standard

(5) **Brand marriages** as joint ventures in appreciation of a worldly image will increasingly make sense to partners who share common long-term values and enjoy learning from each other.

Brand marriages

Disney/Nestlé: 'One focal idea instead of 1000 new ideas' explained Nestlés exclusive rights to Disney characters on food products in Europe.

Benetton/Barbie: 'Barbie dolls dressed up in Benetton colours.'

---

(6) **Umbrella image barriers** are rapidly becoming as significant forces as classical market entry barriers. Reasons include:
- media fracture
- size of mental territory marked off in crowded consumers' minds
- retailers' own brands

Image subsidiaries
44–6

WHAT IF LUX HAD NOT BEEN
TYPECASTED TO SOAPS ?

(7) **Brand identity systems** now rely on a language instead of a name. The strategic objective is to capitalize on every communications pitch.

Branding's 3rd base
63–8

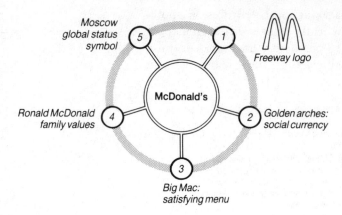

Opportunities of brand languages:

- multiple designs
  - media channels
  - points of sale
  - usage occasions
  - consumers' identities
- moving vocabularies
  - brand stretching
  - multiple global entry points
  - licensing component symbols

Risks of brand languages:

- legal protection
- can be a complex investment to coordinate

(8) **Risk concentration** The larger the goodwill invested in a single entity (billion dollar brands are no longer rarities), the more important audits of future environmental scenarios become. A brand range can be as strong as its weakest link.

The symbol 88–91

Global headlines 4–6

Edge 51

The tree of life 140–53

> '*Perrier's ghost remains because it branded the product category as being purer than pure*'

(9) **Under-branded companies** should note the property right which branders aim to own, namely all the goodwill created by the value-added chain:

- The opportunities to brand dominant marketing positions on a world stage may never be more favourable than the 1990s.
- The double irony is to manufacture a world class product under contract to someone else's brand (for example, historically several Marks & Spencer's suppliers including Courtaulds Textiles).

> The owner of the communications link claims the property right

... the added value chain ...

Product development
Manufacture
Distribution
Communications
Store location
Shop designs
Merchandising display

(10) **World class brands** are communications channels. The target is to become personally identified with the magnetism of leadership.

3 creative questions 36–40

Journalistic criteria	Market competitor
● size	● differentiated focus
● symbolic immediacy || News	● consistency of style
● fashionability	● intensity of investment
	● coherent trading partnerships

Worthy

Transnational corporate trends 57–8

- Premium pricing (long term) and low cost
- Humanity of branded goods – product and corporate
- Understanding global aspiration and local touch

Triad reorganization 82–4

In summary, in our era of televisual images for cosmopolitan consumption, we should no longer be surprised that internationally recognized stereotypes are property rights which carry a

Corporate PR and brand identity are merging
as one force

All the world's
a stage
for example, McDonald's
Moscow opening

Many audiences
are listening
for example, the staff
mission in BA's
message as the
world's favourite
airline

Transnational
communications
strategies aim to
make national
brands parochial

substantial premium. Today's most creative marketing plans involve reorganizing the ways famous brands are presented to leverage business opportunities. As the change from a parochial to an international world accelerates, world class branders are linking up marketing platforms within a company's operational domain and linking companies through branded alliances to a franchise which identifies a global quality standard with a cosmopolitan lifestyle.

Selected Reading List

Advertising

Harrison, A. *A Handbook of Advertising Techniques*. Kogan Page, 1987
Mayer, M. *Madison Avenue, USA*. Penguin, 1961
Ogilvy, D. *Confessions of an Advertising Man*. Pan, 1987
Reeves, R. *Advertising Reality*. A.A. Knopf, 1986
Watkins, J. *The 100 Greatest Advertisements*. Dover, 1959
Young, J.W. *How to Become an Advertising Man*. Advertising Publications, 1963

Business/Management

Buzzell, R. and Gale, B. *The PIMS Principles*. The Free Press, 1987
The Economist. Surveys – The Year of the Brand; Punters or Proprietors?
Waterman, R. *The Renewal Factor*. Bantam, 1987
  plus all works by Drucker, P., Heller, R. and Porter, M.

Company biographies

Morita, A. *Made in Japan (Sony)*. E.P. Dutton, 1986
Palazzini, F. *Coco-Cola Superstar*. Columbus Books, 1989
Tse, K. *Marks & Spencer*. Pergamon, 1987

Design/Communications Identities

Itten, J. *The Elements of Colour*. Van Nostrand Reinhold, 1986
Morgan, H. *Symbols of America*. Penguin, 1987
Murphy, J. and Rowe, M. *How to Design Trademarks and Logos*. Phaidon, 1988
Olins, W. *Corporate Identity*. Thames & Hudson, 1989

Marketing

Davidson, J.H. *Offensive Marketing*. Pelican, 1975

Jones, J. *What's in a Name?* Gower, 1986

Levitt, T. *The Marketing Imagination*. The Free Press, 1986

Ries, A. and Trout, J. *Positioning – the battle for your mind*. McGraw-Hill, 1981

Urban, G. and Hauser, R. *The Design and Marketing of New Products*. Prentice Hall, 1980

Society/History (past and future)

Benedict, R. *The Chrysanthemum and The Sword*. Charles E. Tuttle, 1985

Hobsbawm, E. and Ranger, T. *The Invention of Tradition*. Cambridge University Press, 1988

Macrae, N. *The 2024 Report: a concise history of the future*. Sidgwick & Jackson, 1984

McLuhan, M. *Understanding Media*. Ark Paperbacks 1987

Naisbitt, J. and Aburdene, P. *Megatrends 2000*. Sidgwick & Jackson, 1990

Ohmae, K. *The Borderless World*. Collins, 1990

The broad social compass of world class branding makes any reading list personal and partial. Enjoy broad-casting yours.

Brand Index

General Index